Seeds
Growing with God
Planting Season
by
Vincent R. Faulkner

Kings of Christ

 TRILOGY

Seeds: Growing with God. Planting Season

Trilogy Christian Publishers A Wholly Owned Subsidary of Trinity Broadcasting Network

2442 Michelle Drive Tustin, CA 92780

Scripture quotations marked KJV are taken from the King James Version of the Bible. Public domain.

No part of this book may be reproduced, stored in a retrieval system, or transmitted by any means without written permission from the author. All rights reserved. Printed in the USA.

Rights Department, 2442 Michelle Drive, Tustin, CA 92780.

Trilogy Christian Publishing/TBN and colophon are trademarks of Trinity Broadcasting Network.

Cover design by: Vincent R. Faulkner

For information about special discounts for bulk purchases, please contact Trilogy Christian Publishing.

Trilogy Disclaimer: The views and content expressed in this book are those of the author and may not necessarily reflect the views and doctrine of Trilogy Christian Publishing or the Trinity Broadcasting Network.

Manufactured in the United States of America

10 9 8 7 6 5 4 3 2 1

Library of Congress Cataloging-in-Publication Data is available.

ISBN: 978-1-64773-271-4

E-ISBN: 978-1-64773-272-1

And hath made us kings and priests unto God and his Father; to him be glory and dominion for ever and ever. Amen.

Revelation 1:6 (KJV)

DEDICATION

Whether you are a Christian or have never met Jesus, you are the reason this book was created. We are all sinners; we are all broken, and we are all the same. We are all like most of the people who will need to read this book to bring themselves closer to God or meet Him for the first time. So, you become the person God intended you to be, and together, we can save the world for His glory.

Thank You, God the Father. Thank You, God the Son. Thank You, God the Holy Spirit. Thank You, Abba. Thank You, Elohim. Thank You, Yahweh. Thank You, El Elyon. Thank You, El Roi. Thank You, El Shaddai. Thank You, Jehovah. Thank You, Messiah. Thank You, Lord and Savior. Thank You, Jesus Christ. Thank You, Alpha and Omega.

Thank You, "I AM"!

ACKNOWLEDGMENTS

My deepest thanks, gratitude, and love go to God the Father, the Son, and the Holy Spirit that provided me with the gift to create this book. I could not be more blessed, humbled, and honored by the Lord and Savior than to be a small part of even one person growing closer to God and finding their way home where they belong with Jesus Christ by reading this book. I pray I will see you in the kingdom of heaven with Him.

Always displaying an amazing example of living as a child of God and being a continuous blessing in my life, my wife is a true soldier of faith, seeing and believing that God is present and purposeful in bringing others to Him through the creation of the messages in this book.

God brought one of His warriors into my life, introducing Bishop Wade Jackson of Philadelphia, PA, of Keep It Real Ministry, who saw in me what God already knew as we took up the cross together. As we continue serving in our mission, we are amazed to watch God at work, blessing the bishop's ministry and many others through following the calling God set in front of us.

TABLE OF CONTENTS

PREFACE

In today's world, Christians and people who have never met God need to be reached in a new way. Everything is instant information with vastly decreasing attention spans to focus and concentrate on what you should be feeding into your mind, body, and soul. Therefore, *Seeds: Growing with God* of Kings of Christ Ministry was created by sharing inspired insight from the ministry minutes of Kings of Christ as a means to introduce Jesus Christ in new different ways to Christians and those that have not met Him yet.

Today, because of the pandemic and many other issues in our world, so much of the focus of our world is on the problem and not the solution. The solution is God and growing your relationship with Him deeper inside of you and bringing others to meet Him for the first time. The more of His children are brought home, and the deeper our relationship is with Him, the better our world will become. He will always provide the way for solutions, but only if each one of us presses into our relationship with Him as His child.

In this book, God has placed a path for you to discover a deeper relationship with Him or meet Him for the very first time. This comes through Him sharing His Word and helping you realize, commit to, and follow through with decisions to bring you closer to the Father as His child. As you read, you will be learning how to open yourself up to the Word of God and the love He has for you. Understanding your true calling is now guiding you to what God has planned for your best eternal life.

Most importantly, we will be going through this journey together. Your personal transformation, because of you reading these words, is reborn every time you read and reread each seed to plant God in you to grow for eternity. It is very simple. (If you keep doing the same things you have been doing and keep expecting different results in life, you will just remain walking around the wilderness instead of conquering your mountains and finding your promised land.) Sometimes this will go on for a lifetime for some people, who never discover what they were designed for, and they don't know why they would never reach what God intended for them.

We are all given a purpose that is only guided by God and followed through with by ourselves. The one question is: Will you give yourself the opportunity to start becoming the person God intended you to be?

> To put off your old self, which belongs to your former manner of life and is corrupt through deceitful desires, and to be renewed in the spirit of your minds, and to put on the new self, created after the likeness of God in true righteousness and holiness.
>
> Ephesians 4:22–24

During this journey, you will walk through the discovery of who you were, who you are now, and who you really want to be and can become. Open your heart, mind, and soul to direct life-changing honesty backed with biblical principles and reap the everlasting rewards of doing so in your life and in the lives of others, growing closer to God or meeting Him for the first time.

You will discover how exciting spiritual growth can be when you become who you really are as a child of God. You must, with intense desire, allow your walls to fall and open your heart, mind, and soul to the Father, the Son, and the Holy Spirit. No excuses, no exceptions: you must commit yourself to God and those that you love—now, not tomorrow, not next week, not next year—now!

This book moves you toward the blessings of eternal life God has in store for you as His child.

Who should own and read this book?

Anyone who has never met Jesus who wants to repent and be forgiven of their sins to be saved through Jesus Christ for eternal life in the kingdom of heaven.

> "But seek first the kingdom of God and his righteousness, and all these things will be added to you" (Matthew 6:33).

Any sinner: anyone who continually violates the Word and commandments of God, who lives their life according to worldly values.

> "If we confess our sins, he is faithful and just to forgive us our sins and to cleanse us from all unrighteousness" (1 John 1:9).

Any believer who wants to plant seeds of God to grow closer to Him to become who He intends them to be as His child.

WHAT IS THE GOSPEL? (GOOD NEWS)

As we begin our journey through the Bible, we are to discover what the gospel is. Why does the gospel matter? How does it affect your eternal life as a child of God? We will also learn what you should know about it.

First, let's make sure we understand what the gospel is and what the gospel means. Do you know what the gospel is? Do you know what the gospel means?

The gospel is a message of good news from God.

There seem to be many versions of how the gospel is perceived, but what does it really mean from a Christian point of view? We have learned to this point that the gospel means the good news about Jesus Christ. But what about Jesus Christ being the good news? It is actually a combination of several things, which is the birth, death, and resurrection of Jesus Christ. But it is also about the kingdom of heaven that was created for you to spend eternity in by being saved through Jesus. The greatest thing about the gospel is that God gives you a choice to have eternal life instead of death in the world. He provides you with a guaranteed escape from death and a path to Him through His Son so that you don't have to be lost. God also makes sure to share His Word with you in a way you clearly understand the results of how your decisions affect your life as His child here on the earth and in heaven.

It is the map with directions for your true destiny. It is the key to the doors of the kingdom of heaven, blessings, and eternal life with the Father through the Son and the Holy Spirit.

The gospel is perceived as the saving acts of God due to the work of His Son, Jesus, on the cross and Jesus's resurrection from the dead, which brings reconciliation between His children and God.

Now, let's expand on the blessings of God's Word.

What does "the gospel is perceived" mean?

"To have perceived" or "to perceive the gospel" means you have now become aware of, know, identify by means of the senses and understanding of something. You can no longer deny its existence or that you are unaware because you have now gained knowledge and wisdom.

What are the "saving acts of God"?

The sacrifice of His only Son, Jesus Christ, to wash away your sins and give you eternal life in the kingdom of heaven.

What is "due to the work of His Son, Jesus, on the cross"?

The crucifixion that Jesus suffered to save everyone from sin and provide eternal life in the kingdom of heaven to all those who are believers.

How do you explain Jesus's resurrection from the dead?

We are all born again when we become new believers and followers of the Word of God through the Son, Jesus Christ. We are all resurrected in eternal life, which brings reconciliation between His children and God: we are now saved through the Son to have a relationship with the Father as His children.

We just learned what the gospel is and that it means good news about Jesus. But why is the gospel considered to be good news? In reality, ever since the good news about Jesus Christ was announced, from the beginning, it has brought on many questions about our entire existence. Where do we even find the answers to everything we want to know about our entire existence and how it relates to the good news and Jesus? The Bible, since its creation, has been used to provide a form of explanation to all of these questions: why we exist, who and what we are, how we should live our lives in order to find salvation, and what might happen if we choose another direction. You quickly learn, once you understand what the good news is, that nobody wants to be left behind once they discover the good news. God's word in the Bible clearly spells out what is required of you as His child for you to be with Him in heaven, where He is always waiting for you.

What should you know about the good news?

The first thing to know about the good news of Jesus is that "in the beginning, God created the heavens and the earth" (Genesis 1:1). Everything started from that point, so if you get that point wrong, then everything else that follows will be wrong as well.

Because God created everything—including us—He has the right to tell us how to live as His children and what He expects from us. Plus, just like normal children, if we choose a different path than His instructions in His Word, then you can expect correction to come your way so you can be who God intends you to be as His child.

You have to understand that in order to understand the good news about Jesus. To understand just how glorious and life-giving the gospel of Jesus Christ is, we have to understand that God is also holy and righteous. He is determined never to ignore or tolerate sin. Including ours!

Do you know what the purpose of the gospel creation is?

There's no greater assignment in life than being a servant to God and sharing the gospel of Jesus Christ. The gospel is not intended to save civilization from wreckage but to save people from the wreckage of civilization. This is worth hearing again, so let me repeat this to you: the gospel is not intended to save civilization from destruction but to save people from the destruction of civilization.

Now that we have learned what the gospel is, let's answer a few questions:

Are you ashamed or embarrassed about the gospel?

Are you ashamed or embarrassed to put a Bible in your car or at work?

Are you ashamed to invite people to meet Jesus Christ or to your church services?

We absolutely should be open and bold for the gospel of our Lord and Savior Jesus Christ as He was for us. His name is above every name.

How can we be ashamed of the gospel when the power of the gospel is the only thing that can save this world? The gospel is the only thing that can make alcoholics and drug addicts sober. It is the only thing that can make adulterers and fornicators pure. It is the only thing that can give you real hope that is steadfast and true.

Without the gospel of Jesus Christ, there is no hope. There is only one power that can wash us and make us whiter than snow, and that is the power of the gospel. It is by grace through faith.

The ways of the world can only be a better place to go to hell from.

This world looks to its own creations to save us and not the creations of God. The gospel is the only true saving grace to eternal life for a child of God and who He intends him or her to be.

One of the most important commitments you can make as a Christian is to read your Bible every day. In each message, we will provide you with a few scriptures to look up and read on your own to plant seeds inside of you for a deeper understanding so you can grow closer to Jesus Christ through His written word.

It's time to get your Bible. For your growing with God, scriptures for "What Is the Gospel?" are Romans 1:16, 1 Corinthians 15:1–4, and Mark 1:15.

I pray that this message creates a path for you to grow closer to Jesus Christ or meet Him for the first time. If you want to receive the guaranteed passage that He sacrificed Himself on the cross for so you can be saved as a child of God, then become who you are created to be and turn the words you read in this book into action now so you can have eternal life in the kingdom of heaven that is just waiting for you.

Planting Notes:

_____

_____

_____

_____

_____

HELLO, GOD: ASK, SEEK, AND KNOCK

Let's continue our journey through the Bible. In our next message, you will discover how to ask, seek, and knock to request God's attention, what you should know about it, and how it affects your eternal life as a child of God. "Ask, and it will be given to you; seek, and you will find; knock, and it will be opened to you" (Matthew 7:7).

How does God hear you when you ask for His help?

Asking is a verbal connection to God.

➢ First, understand God will hear your prayers whether you are a follower of Jesus or not. But if you want Him to really hear you, you need to have a relationship with God and read His Word. Keep in mind, as part of your request, God may ask something of you as well, and you should follow His request.

Remember: when you ask for something from God, it's like Him getting a phone call from someone He does not know or from His child. He may answer both of them, but one will be far more intently listened to. It is also important to be honest and specific about what you are asking God for clear understanding.

How do you seek God?

Seeking is a mind connection to God.

➢ The seeking of God is the conscious effort to go through our natural means as His child to reach God Himself, to constantly set our minds toward God in everything we do at all times, to direct our minds and hearts toward Him through the means of His revelation. This is what "to seek God" means.

The four scriptural references in the Bible you need to follow to seek God include *priorities*, *prayer*, *humility*, and *surrender*.

Priorities are a matter of the *heart*. Jesus told the crowd, if they are thirsty, to come to Him (John 7:37). The greatest pursuit of your life begins when you set your heart to seek after God first always. When His presence becomes your greatest desire, you are headed in the right direction and have your priorities in order as He expects from you as His child.

Prayer. You cannot have a personal relationship with someone you aren't willing to communicate with. Read God's Word and ask Him for a greater understanding of His will for you as His child. Remember: you can pray for anything you want, but you must pray that God's will be done over all that you pray about.

Humility. Jesus once told a story of two men who were praying in the Temple. One man was a religious leader, a Pharisee who lived by a strict religious code. The other was a man who was a dishonest tax collector grieved by his sinfulness. Notice the major differences in the prayers of the two men:

The Pharisee prayed, "God, I thank you that I am not like other men, extortionists, unjust, adulterers, or even as this tax collector. I fast twice a week; I give tithes of all that I possess" (Luke 18:11–12). Notice how he degraded the other man in his prayer and praised himself for doing what is expected of him as a servant of God and nothing more.

The sinner prayed, "God, be merciful to me, a sinner!" (Luke 18:13). Notice there was repentance in his words, asking God to lead him to whom He knows he is supposed to become even if he, the tax collector, must suffer correction to do so, and the Pharisee acted like there was nothing he could do to be more like Jesus.

Of these two men, which do you believe touched the heart of God and received living water? If you answered, "The humble sinner," you are correct. "Everyone who exalts himself will be humbled, and he who humbles himself will be exalted" (Luke 14:11).

Surrender. The Scriptures call us to this: "Draw near to God, and he will draw near to you. Cleanse your hands, sinners, and purify your hearts, you double-minded" (James 4:8).

You must lay everything down to God, give up your total will and control, and allow God to guide you through His will for you as His child by His Word. The ways of the world no longer are heard by you, only the Word of God and His will for your eternal life.

"Knock" is a physical connection to God caused by an action.

Jesus then said, "Knock, and it [the door] will be opened to you" (Matthew 7:7; hereinafter, brackets added for clarity). Here, the Lord uses a metaphor for the action a desire produces. If a person needs something from someone behind a door, the most natural thing to do is knock—and keep knocking until the door is opened and the desire is met. In the same way, a believer should pray in faith for God's provision and be persistent in prayer, knocking at God's door.

Now we will review "asking, seeking, and knocking" to request God's attention. Notice the three different senses being considered here. Asking is verbal; Christians are to use their mouths and petition God for their needs and desires. And believers are to seek with their minds—this is more than asking; it is a setting of priorities and a focusing of the heart. To knock involves physical movement, one in which the Christian takes action. Although asking and seeking are of great importance, they would be incomplete without knocking.

One of the most important commitments you can make as a Christian is to read your Bible every day. In each message, we will provide you with a few scriptures to look up and read on your own

to plant seeds inside of you for a deeper understanding so you can grow closer to Jesus Christ.

It's time to get your Bible. For your growing with God, scriptures for how to ask, seek, and knock to request God's attention are Matthew 21:22, Luke 11:9–13, and Jeremiah 29:13.

I pray that this message creates a path for you to grow closer to Jesus Christ or meet Him for the first time. If you want to receive the guaranteed passage that He sacrificed Himself on the cross for so you could be saved as a child of God, then become who you are created to be and turn the words you read in this book into action now so you can have eternal life in the kingdom of heaven that is just waiting for you.

Planting Notes:

_____

_____

_____

_____

_____

GOD'S ARMOR

In our next message on this journey through the Bible, we will reveal how God's armor is your invincible shield of protection and path of promise forever. You will become aware of what you should know and how God's armor affects your eternal life as a child of God.

Are you prepared for battle? If you are a Christian, you should be every day. Do you have your shield and your sword? Do you have your body armor on? Are your steps straight and true? Is your mind an impenetrable fortress? Do your words defend who you are as a child of God? Does your soul burn so bright it lights the way for you and others to take up the cross?

What is the most important gift God gave you to defeat the sin of the world besides Jesus? What is the map that has already been written for you to follow that leads directly to salvation? Where are the battle plans written to defeat any war that comes up against you? If you are going to war, you must have a battle plan for any situation that will lead you to victory. Do you have a plan for guaranteed victory?

All of us should be ready to battle for God as a soul champion for Christ every day that He gives us; our first purpose is to serve. You are His warrior, and with that, you have the almighty power of God inside of you to defeat all evil that comes against you.

With great power comes great responsibility to follow, as God commands His soldiers of faith to bring Him back the wounded and the lost from the battlefield every day so He may heal His children.

By now, I am sure you have discovered that we are talking about the Word of God, the written word of life in the Bible, the perfect plan for any situation. It is the armor of life that defeats your enemies from all directions, in all ways, at all times.

The plans that are provided to you are so important that you are to read, memorize, internalize, and share them with others to ensure the plans for the secret of salvation and eternal life will be there for those today and for all future generations to come until He arrives again.

So, the plans will never disappear or be lost from the world so others may find their way out of the battlefield into the fields of glory with the almighty Lord and Savior who is, who was, and who will forever be through His word in the Scriptures.

We can find many examples of how important it is for you to know the Word of God and wear His armor daily in everything you do. Let's look at scriptures about knowing the Word of God and being an unstoppable force for the good of all through Christ.

We will start with the scripture of Matthew 4:1–4:

> Then Jesus was led by the Spirit into the wilderness to be tempted by the devil. After fasting forty days and forty nights, Jesus was very hungry. The tempter came to him [thinking he was weak] and said, "If you are the Son of God, tell these stones to become bread." Jesus answered, "It is written: 'Man shall not live on bread alone, but on every word that comes from the mouth of God.'"

This shows you the fortitude of Christ that even while He was starving and weak, the Word of God fed Him more than anything that exists in the world or that Satan could ever offer. The food of eternal life is fed through your heart, mind, and soul so that you will never experience hunger or temptation when you know His Word and your actions honor the Holy Father and the Son to become who He intends you to be.

It is obvious that you must have the armor of God on to go to battle for the kingdom. If you are not willing to take up the cross and the written Word daily and become a soul soldier through the power of Christ in you, you will more than likely experience wounds that will never heal from war after war in your life that may even take your last breath, bypassing salvation, to suffer a dishonorable death.

Now let's look at the scripture of Matthew 4:5–7 (NIV).

> Then the devil took him to the holy city and had him stand on the highest point of the temple. "If you are the Son of God," he said, "throw yourself down. For it is written: 'He will command his angels concerning you, and they will lift you up in their hands, so that you will not strike your foot against a stone.'" Jesus answered him, "It is also written: 'Do not put the Lord your God to the test.'"

Jesus once again shows us that the power of the Word of God has defeated Satan. As Jesus spoke with His sword of the truth, no enemy shall even rise up against you. There is no gray area in the Word of God, as the truth has no waiver or fear. So you see that Satan uses many words to try to distract and redirect you, to place confusion within you, and God's Word is clear, direct, and concise.

Let us look at our last scripture in this message, Matthew 4:8–11 (NIV):

> Again, the devil took him to a very high mountain and showed him all the kingdoms of the world and their splendor. "All this I will give you," he said, "if you will bow down and worship me." Jesus said to him, "Away from me, Satan! For it is written: 'Worship the Lord your God, and serve him only.'" Then the devil left him, and angels came and attended to him.

As a final thought: you can see Satan will try to lead you around everywhere, trying to weaken you so he can crack the armor of God that you have. Understand that God's armor is a fortress around your heart, mind, and soul. Satan will try to defeat you in any of these areas, so you must constantly shine and clean your armor by reading the word of God daily in your Bible.

Not only must you read the Word of God, but you must also know it to the point of instant recall to activate your immediate defense system against the enemies of your Father. You must wear your armor of God everywhere you go and in all that you do. You must be prepared for battle at any moment and be ready for surprise attacks.

But most importantly, you must allow your armor of God to shine so others may see the power of the Almighty in you that they can have through salvation in Jesus Christ. Remember to read your Bible, as God is always watching you; put on the armor He has there to protect you because He loves you so very much.

One of the most important commitments you can make as a Christian is to read your Bible every day. In each message, we will provide you with a few scriptures to look up and read on your own to plant seeds inside of you for a deeper understanding so you can grow closer to Jesus Christ through His written word.

It's time to get your Bible. For your growing with God, scriptures for "God's Armor" are Ephesians 6:10–18, Isaiah 59:17, and Revelation 19:1–21.

I pray that this message creates a path for you to grow closer to Jesus Christ or meet Him for the first time. If you want to receive the guaranteed passage that He sacrificed Himself on the cross for so you can be saved as a child of God, then become who you are created to be and turn the words you read in this book into action now so you can have eternal life in the kingdom of heaven that is just waiting for you.

Planting Notes:

_____

_____

_____

_____

_____

THE BREATH OF GOD

As we continue down a new path through the Bible, we will learn how the breath of God is the only air you need to breathe. It purifies your mind, body, and soul as only God can do. You will experience everlasting joy and well-being as you become aware of what you should know and how the breath of God affects your eternal life as a child of God.

So, to begin, do you know what the breath of God is? What does it do? How does it affect you? Should you be concerned if you don't know what the breath of God is?

Can you even imagine something so powerful as the breath of God that breathes life into existence? Let's get a better understanding of how the breath of God began as He chose the vessels of His written word to record and speak the breath of God.

All of us have been chosen to have the most important power God gave His Son because we are His children and made in His likeness in every way. Therefore, you should take your every breath in life through Jesus Christ and His will and not your own free will, which can lead to the suffocation of your soul. Living through His Word pleases God, and ultimately, you are to breathe life into others with His Word, which is God's greatest desire.

Do you know until you are saved and God has filled you full of His breath that you have never really been alive until that moment? Do you know His breath is like oxygen to your soul? We all know what happens when you stop breathing oxygen: you dwindle into nothingness and become empty and lifeless and then die in life and spirit.

Until you are born again, you are living on an oxygen tank that will run out and never can be filled again, called "the world," that only leads to your suffocation ending in the death of your life and soul. But good news! You can bypass death and head straight to eternal life the second you take your first breath through God and His Word.

So, have you figured it out yet? Do you know what the breath of God is? It is the only thing that you will ever need to have the life you were created for. It is the Word of God, the Bible.

The second you speak the Word of God, whether you are reading it out loud or sharing it with others, leading them to know Jesus, you are experiencing the breath of God coming through you as His true disciple and child.

Let's explore some scriptures teaching us about the breath of God in His Word of life. First, we will visit the beginning with Genesis 2:7: "Then the LORD God formed the man of dust from the ground and breathed into his nostrils the breath of life, and the man became a living creature." We see that the breath of God creates life from dust that was the birth of man and all living things.

Now let's visit more Scripture with 2 Timothy 3:16: "All Scripture is breathed out by God and profitable for teaching, for reproof, for correction, and for training in righteousness." This is incredible that God is telling us how to breathe in and exhale His breath through us and use it for what He desires when He speaks His written Word.

Next, we will look at the scripture of Job 33:4: "The Spirit of God has made me, and the breath of the Almighty gives me life." This is to tell us that you realize the Holy Spirit is what you are made of and life is given to you by the breath of God.

We will continue with Job 32:8 (NLT): "But there is a spirit within people, the breath of the Almighty within them, that makes them intelligent." Now we are learning that others can see the breath of God in His children because of who you are and how you act, think, and speak, as He intended you to be glorifying His name and kingdom.

Moving on to the scripture of Job 27:3–4 (NLT): "As long as I live, while I have the breath from God, my lips will speak no evil, and my tongue will speak no lies." This verse is so pleasing to God, as He knows that you are His child through your commitment to live your life by following His Word in all areas.

The next scripture we are visiting is Psalm 104:29–30 (NLT):

> But if you turn away from them, they panic. When you take away their breath, they die and turn again to dust. When you give them your breath, life is created, and you renew the face of the earth.

If God has placed His breath in you, but you continue to sin and not follow or read His Word, then you will feel His breath slip from your life as you are heading down the path of the lost. So you must remember when the breath of God entered you that you were born again to carry the cross throughout the world to save the lost and bring them to Jesus.

Our final scripture in this message paints the picture very clearly about what the breath of God is: "God, the LORD, created the heavens and stretched them out. He created the earth and everything in it. He gives breath to everyone, life to everyone who walks the earth" (Isaiah 42:5, NLT). This verse says it all: that nothing would ever have been created or exist without the breath of God, turning all of existence into life in this entire world, including you.

Our mission is to grow closer to God as we breathe His breath that He placed in us in and out through learning just a few scriptures about the amazing power and blessing that the breath of God has in our lives. Actually, without it, we would not even be alive on a journey of a blessed, filled eternal life in the kingdom of heaven. We would return to dust and eternal death as if we never lived.

So, we now have a deeper knowledge about the breath of God and understand that the breath of God is the Bible and the word of God. It is like your own endless supply of clean and pure oxygen in a world of toxic air that could kill you if you breathe it in and out of your mind, body, or soul, ultimately by passing eternal life and participating in death without it. The choice is yours.

One of the most important commitments you can make as a Christian is to read your Bible every day. In each message, we will provide you with a few scriptures to look up and read on your own to plant seeds inside of you for a deeper understanding so you can grow closer to Jesus Christ through His written Word.

It's time to get your Bible. For your growing with God, scriptures for "The Breath of God" are Psalm 33:6, Hebrews 4:12, and Matthew 4:4.

I pray that this message creates a path for you to grow closer to Jesus Christ or meet Him for the first time. If you want to receive the guaranteed passage that He sacrificed Himself on the cross for so you can be saved as a child of God, then become who you are created to be and turn the words you read in this book into action now so you can have eternal life in the kingdom of heaven that is just waiting for you.

Planting Notes:

_____

_____

_____

_____

_____

Do You Read Your Bible, or Does Your Bible Read You?

In this message, we are approaching an eye-opening perspective most people do not realize in understanding God's Word. Most people believe they are reading a book to learn about Jesus Christ, what He has done for all of us, and how it affects our lives for eternity. When in reality, each word you read in the Bible opens the door for God to explore deeper who you are and begin to show you a path to eternal life with Him that you can have in heaven through Jesus Christ.

Actually, both of those occur within the written Word of God. What happens to you when you read the Bible? What happens to you when the Bible is reading you? Unlike any other book in existence, it has the ability to read you as you read it—what does *that* mean?

Simply put: as you learn the Word of God, the Word of God learns you by becoming a part of who you are through the instruction of an action, usually by God; while you are reading the Bible, you act on your own instruction and free will based on the Word of God.

There are reasons for this. God wants certain things to be very clear in His instruction, and at other times, He wants you to grow from His Word and count on your own instruction through His Word so you can be closer to the likeness and image of the Son, Jesus Christ.

We are going to go through Scripture so you can see the difference between you reading the Bible and the Bible reading you. Almost always, when the Bible is reading you, there is a message from God with clear instructions on what you are supposed to do.

Reading your Bible, on the other hand, is taking in God's word and applying it to your life; you are choosing the way of instruction to yourself through His Word. So, the Bible reading you is giving you instruction, and you reading the Bible is you giving you instruction through the Word. Let's get started and look at some scriptures!

First, let's look at the Bible reading you with Joshua 1:8 that says,

> This Book of the Law shall not depart from your mouth,
> but you shall meditate on it day and night, so that you
> may be careful to do according to all that is written in it.
> For then you will make your way prosperous, and then
> you will have good success.

Do you see it? Clear instructions from God on how you are to follow His Word in this scriptural verse, meaning when you are a child of God, the words you speak will never change and forever be the words of God, and you are to diligently study the word in the Bible and let it be in your thoughts twenty-four hours of every day of your life.

To protect you as His child, He instructs this of you according to His Word. Once you have done this, He has prepared you for the blessings that come with being His child. It is very clear that the Bible is reading you, and as you follow His Word, it allows God to see who you are so you become what He has intended you to be.

Now let's look at the scripture of 1 Timothy 4:13: "Until I come, devote yourself to the public reading of Scripture, to exhortation, to teaching."

Can you guess whether this scripture is the Bible is reading you or you reading the Bible? If you said it was the Bible reading you because you noticed His specific instruction is to direct you to an action He expects of you, then you would be correct.

In this scripture, God is saying, "Until I return again, you are to devote your life to diligently reading and emphatically communicating verbally, out loud, the Word of God, especially to others. You are to share the good news with them for the opportunity to be forgiven and saved so they may know Jesus Christ and to expand the kingdom of heaven by saving one of My children through My Word in you."

We will visit one more scripture in regard to the Bible reading you, Isaiah 41:10: "Fear not, for I am with you; be not dismayed, for I am your God; I will strengthen you, I will help you, I will uphold you with my righteous right hand."

This verse is very clear that God is speaking directly to you with instruction and clarity. He is telling you that He is with you always and that you never need to fear anything because He is always with you. No matter what you have going on in your life, God is there and will never leave your side or abandon you as His child.

Now, let's look at when you are reading the Bible and see what the Scriptures reveal in 2 Timothy 3:16–17: "All Scripture is breathed out by God and profitable for teaching, for reproof, for correction, and for training in righteousness, that the man of God may be competent, equipped for every good work."

Let's expand on this verse, as this is where God is telling you something in His Word He wants you to know. Here He is saying, "My Word comes from Me and is to be used for all the directions for you as My child that you may go in. Following My Word will get you prepared for what I need you in every way for eternal life with Me."

But as you see, He does not instruct you to do something as an action as in the verses before. He is simply stating this is how every-thing works and what the results of following His Word will be. So this is an example of you reading the Bible.

Even though reading the Bible and the Bible reading you will both get you closer to Jesus, the Bible reading you is an instructional change that God wants you to do now, and you reading the Bible is information you must instruct yourself to use according to His Word.

So let's look at another verse where you are reading the Bible, Psalm 119:10–11: "With my whole heart I seek you; let me not wander from your commandments! I have stored up your word in my heart that I might not sin against you."

As you can see, this is very clear that you are reading the Bible, as you are talking to God in this scripture. If you don't know what to pray for, you can always find a verse like this one that you can pray that God lead you to follow His Word in all ways.

In this scripture, you are laying it all down, surrendering everything, and asking God to guide you in a way to glorify Him. You are sharing with God that you have done as He asked and read His Word and understand it. His Word is not only a part of who you are, but it is also who you are as His child, and you do not want to fail Him in any way.

One of the most important commitments you can make as a Christian is to read your Bible every day. In each message, we will provide you with a few scriptures to look up and read on your own to plant seeds inside of you for a deeper understanding so you can grow closer to Jesus Christ through His written word.

It's time to get your Bible. For your growing with God, scriptures for "Do You Read Your Bible, or Does Your Bible Read You?" are Joshua 1:8, Romans 15:4, and Luke 24:45.

I pray that this message creates a path for you to grow closer to Jesus Christ or meet Him for the first time. If you want to receive the guaranteed passage that He sacrificed Himself on the cross for so you can be saved as a child of God, then become who you are created to be and turn the words you read in this book into action now so you can have eternal life in the kingdom of heaven that is just waiting for you.

Planting Notes:

_____

_____

_____

_____

_____

THE POWER OF YOUR PRAYERS

We have now discovered in our journey through the Bible how important embracing the Word of God is to our spiritual life. In this message, we are expanding our commitment to grow in faith through the power of prayer that can change our life and the lives of all those around us. What does prayer mean? Why is it important to God and us? What can happen without prayer and with prayer in our life being a daily priority?

One of the most important parts of your relationship with God is your prayer life. No matter where you are in your prayer life—just beginning or a prayer warrior—prayer allows you to lay your burdens down and let God be there for you in your time of need. Plus, you will discover the greatest blessings in prayer come by praying for others' needs before your own, which brings you closer to God and who He intends you to be.

Let's pray together with our words coming straight from the Bible, from Matthew 6:9–13. Please follow along with the message:

> Pray then like this: "Our Father in heaven, hallowed be
> your name. Your kingdom come, your will be done, on
> earth as it is in heaven. Give us this day our daily bread,
> and forgive us our debts, as we also have forgiven our
> debtors. And lead us not into temptation, but deliver us
> from evil. Amen."

Let's reveal the blessings in God's written Word for a greater understanding!

"Pray then like this" means repeat these words:

"Our Father in heaven": God the Father, God the Son, and God the Holy Spirit in the kingdom of heaven.

"Hallowed be your name": to glorify the name of God as well as God, as they are the same.

"Your kingdom come": through our love of God, we are anticipating the coming of the kingdom of heaven.

"Your will be done": we are acknowledging God's way is best and His will for us is always what we should desire.

"On earth as it is in heaven": God's will we be done here on the earth exactly as it is done in heaven.

"Give us this day our daily bread": we come to God every day to be fed by His Word and spirit.

"And forgive us our debts, as we also have forgiven our debtors": if you forgive others of their sins, your heavenly Father will forgive you of your sins.

"And lead us not into temptation": God guides our steps in such a way that we avoid people and places that can tempt us with evil.

"But deliver us from evil": bring us not into trials but rescue us from all evil and the heart of disbelief.

One of the most important commitments you can make as a Christian is to read your Bible every day. In each message, we will provide you with a few scriptures to look up and read on your own to plant seeds inside of you for a deeper understanding so you can grow closer to Jesus Christ through His written word.

It's time to get your Bible. For your growing with God, scriptures for "The Power of Your Prayers" are James 5:16, 1 Thessalonians 5:17, and 2 Chronicles 7:14.

I pray that this message creates a path for you to grow closer to Jesus Christ or meet Him for the first time. If you want to receive the guaranteed passage that He sacrificed Himself on the cross for so you can be saved as a child of God, then become who you are created to be and turn the words you read in this book into action now so you can have eternal life in the kingdom of heaven that is just waiting for you.

Planting Notes:

_____

_____

_____

_____

_____

How Do You Listen to God?

Now we are going to explore why we were created with two ears and one mouth. We are supposed to listen twice as much as we speak. If you don't listen, then how can you hear? No one cares about how much you know until they know how much you care. Listening is caring. If you are not willing to listen to anyone, then why would you expect them to listen to you? Your ability to listen to others expresses the care you have for them and makes them want to listen to you, just like you listening to God shows Him how much you love Him and makes Him want to listen to you when you need Him.

How do we listen to God?

How do we hear His Word?

How do we know what He wants us to do?

Let's get started with Proverbs 2:1–5 and reveal God's blessings within His Word:

> My son, if you receive my words and treasure up my commandments with you, making your ear attentive to wisdom and inclining your heart to understanding; yes, if you call out for insight and raise your voice for understanding, if you seek it like silver and search for it as for hidden treasures, then you will understand the fear of the LORD and find the knowledge of God.

First, we need to understand that we must read God's Word in order to hear Him when He speaks to us. You need to always be listening for God with your ears, eyes, and soul without a barrier of time or restriction so you do not miss any blessing He has for you.

Otherwise, if you don't know His Word, it is as if you are hearing a foreign language you or God doesn't understand. It is imperative that you internalize His commandments to the point of instant recall and make them a part of your soul as His child.

One of the most important things, in order to hear and listen to God, is that you need to speak God's Word physically with your voice, as this action ingrains His Word inside of you so you can call on Him at any time and He can hear you. You cannot just read it and memorize it.

When you talk to anyone and want them to hear you, the only way to do that is to speak a language they and you can understand. In order to completely immerse yourself in the love of God, you must speak the language of His Word.

You must search for God as if He was a hidden treasure and take in every bit of information to learn from the Father as His child. However, unlike most treasure maps with directions that provide you no guarantee of finding the reward, God has given you the map to find your treasure of salvation and eternal life as His child so that you are who He intends you to be and understand the consequences of correction and blessings by following His Word in your life.

Let's dig a little deeper now with John 8:47: "Whoever is of God hears the words of God. The reason why you do not hear them is that you are not of God."

No matter who you are or where you come from, in order to hear God, you have to surrender yourself to the Lord and Savior to be saved and forgiven. You need to become familiar with God's voice so that you know when you hear His voice as you would your father's. As He is.

By committing yourself to the Lord and Savior, you will never perish, and no one will snatch you out of His hand of never-ending love, mercy, grace, forgiveness, or your salvation with Him in the kingdom of heaven.

Listen carefully; this is important, so you don't want to miss it. If you have not given yourself to the Savior, read His Word, followed

His Word, and spoken His Word into your life and that of others, then how can you expect Him to hear you, as He does not know you and you do not know Him?

Let's continue with the scripture of Psalm 37:4–5: "Delight yourself in the LORD, and he will give you the desires of your heart. Commit your way to the LORD; trust in him, and he will act."

Not only do you need to read, speak, and act on God's Word, you need to find and know the joy and peace that comes with being a child of God.

If you do this, then God will hear you and what your heart desires are and will give them to you—in His time and not yours. This is where your unlimited faith sets a lighted path straight to the Father, the Son, and the Holy Spirit.

Since your heart's first desire should always be God and your relationship with the Father, the Son, and the Holy Spirit, by placing His Word as your first priority, you create the desire for God to cover your life in blessings forever as His child who listens and follows His Word. In turn, you will always find an audience with Him available when you need Him.

You must, without waiver, dedicate your life to the Lord and know that His way is always the best way and the right way for your life at that moment. You must always trust in God no matter what is happening with everything in your life, and He will act on it if you have done what He expects of you as His child.

We will conclude this message with Revelation 3:20: "Behold, I stand at the door and knock. If anyone hears my voice and opens the door, I will come in to him and eat with him, and he with me."

Let's realize God is always, always, *always* waiting for you; He is always trying to get your attention because you are His child; He has never-ending patience with you, and He has given you the key to open the door to come home when He calls for you.

If you use the key He gave you to open the door to be with Him, then you have guaranteed yourself salvation and eternal life in the kingdom of heaven through the Son to the Father, filled with only the kind of love that a father can give the child he loves. So, you can become who He intends you to be in life as His miracle.

One of the most important commitments you can make as a Christian is to read your Bible every day. In each message, we will provide you with a few scriptures to look up and read on your own to plant seeds inside of you for a deeper understanding so you can grow closer to Jesus Christ through His written word.

It's time to get your Bible. For your growing with God, scriptures for "How Do You Listen to God?" are James 1:19, John 8:12, and Ecclesiastes 12:13.

I pray that this message creates a path for you to grow closer to Jesus Christ or meet Him for the first time. If you want to receive the guaranteed passage that He sacrificed Himself on the cross for so you can be saved as a child of God, then become who you are created to be and turn the words you read in this book into action now so you can have eternal life in the kingdom of heaven that is just waiting for you.

Planting Notes:

_____

_____

_____

_____

_____

The Number One Way to Please God

As humans, because we are made in God's image, we desire to please others to express that we care for them and what they think and how they feel. Pleasing someone can be a physical or emotional action, but most importantly, it makes others know you care for them and causes them to care for you more. Why? Because pleasing someone is a form of love they and you both feel when the action of pleasing someone occurs. There is no greater way to show God you love Him than to please Him in your every action and word.

The first thing we need to understand is that the Bible is the most powerful book ever written or that ever will be written. It can save the sinner and motivate the saved to save the souls of others, leading them to know Jesus Christ.

Jesus calls every Christian to step out in faith and spread the good news. The gospel brings good tidings to everyone who will hear it. It offers eternal life to everyone who believes. We, as Christians, are compelled to obey this commandment.

It is the great commission of who we are as children of God. We are designed solely to win the souls of the lost. It is Jesus's command to all His followers and disciples to spread His teachings to all the nations of the world. It is a personal instruction from Jesus and a special calling to His disciples. So, saving souls is not just, "Hey, do you want to go to church with me?" or "Here, I got this Bible for you so you can read it"—to save souls means you invest your time in others as God does for others, and as He did in you to get you on your path to eternal life.

Understand that no matter what strong, God-inspired warrior you are, you always must seek spiritual guidance from God and others. You are a vessel of the Word without limits, sharing the Holy Spirit.

You will never know all the knowledge there is to know and experience about God's wonderful blessings and wisdom because we are all unworthy and there is only one all-seeing and knowing Lord and Savior.

So, do you know what scriptures inspire you to share your faith in Christ? Every Christian should know at least some powerful scriptures so that he or she knows what God expects of him or her. Let's get something clear, and that is your sole purpose: it is to bring souls to Christ once you are saved, or even if you're not saved yet, but the seed of God has been planted in you, just sharing that with others may bring them to want to know Jesus just as you did.

Since winning souls is more important to God than anything you will ever do and is the highest calling that God expects of you as His child, it is your sole purpose when you are saved: to save others. How do you go about doing that? If you are saved and you don't bring others to Christ, will you lose your salvation? Do you know? Do you know how to bring up the topic of Jesus Christ to anyone? Do you know how to save someone's soul and lead them to Jesus Christ?

We are going to explore scriptures that remind us of Christ's command for us to share the gospel and the urgency of our commission. Souls hang in the balance. All of His children and your brothers and sisters are at risk of death, bypassing eternal life. You need to focus and meditate upon these scriptures, and they will provoke you to surrender to obedience and the action of bringing others to the kingdom of heaven with you.

Once you get over the initial fear of sharing your faith, you will be forever grateful that you won souls to Christ and wonder why you didn't do it earlier. Remember everything happens in God's perfect timing. Let's get started with the scripture of Daniel 12:3 (NASB): "Those who have insight will shine brightly like the brightness of the expanse of heaven, and those who lead the many to righteousness, like the stars forever and ever."

This scripture is showing you that if you know the Word of God, the light inside of you (the Lord and Savior) will be noticed and shine for others to see as far away as the stars and will do so for eternity.

He will be waiting for you in heaven, but if you lead others to know Jesus Christ, then you are building the rewards of His blessings abundantly, as you are expanding His kingdom of heaven and leading His children to salvation.

Let's look at the scripture of Romans 10:1 (NASB): "Brethren, my heart's desire and my prayer to God for them is for their salvation." This scripture speaks clearly that your heart is to desire and pray to God for the salvation of all others, always.

Moving on to the scripture of Matthew 28:19 (KJV): "Go ye therefore, and teach all nations, baptizing them in the name of the Father, and of the Son, and of the Holy Ghost." In this scripture, we are learning that God expects all of His children throughout the world to lead souls to be saved through the Word of the Father, the Son, and the Holy Spirit.

As we continue with the scripture of Jude 1:23 (NASB): "Save others, snatching them out of the fire; and on some have mercy with fear, hating even the garment polluted by the flesh." In this verse, we are instructed to bring others to Jesus no matter where they are in life. It should always be any acquaintances in your life that you reach out to. But the ones that are not acquaintances and no one notices or doesn't reach out to will always find a place in the heart of a true soul champion for God to grow His kingdom in heaven.

We are not intended to be alone while we are here or in eternity. Each individual is a dwelling of faith, and each of us must fill his or her portion of the responsibility that is part of being saved as His child. Each individual must be diligent in performing his or her duty of sharing the path of salvation with others, whether enemy or friend.

Let's understand clearly that we only have the power to show others how they can obtain salvation through obedience to the Word of God. We can show others how to walk in order to be saved, for we have the right to do that; we have knowledge and understanding as to how to do it, and it is our privilege to teach it…by being an example of Christ among others wherever we are in the world. But the only person who can truly bring you to Christ is you.

God loves souls so much He sent His only Son, Jesus, as a living sacrifice to take the punishment for our sins. The Bible makes it clear that God loved us first. There is nothing God values more highly than people's souls because they are His children that will be saved and will enter His kingdom where He has already prepared a place for them and for you.

We love God because He first loved us, and in loving God, we need to love others. There is a huge need to share the love of God among all people, for we need to hear the truth that God doesn't want anyone to die or perish! But instead, He desires for everyone to come to Him in repentance for salvation and eternal life that is just waiting for us.

Our mission is to save, preserve from evil, exalt mankind, bring light and truth into the world, prevail upon the people of the earth to walk righteously before God, and honor Him in their lives.

Our purpose is to save the world, save mankind, bring them into harmony with the laws of God and with principles of righteousness, justice, and truth that they may be saved in the kingdom of our God.

We will not finish our work until we have saved ourselves, and then—not until we have saved all depending upon us, for we are to become saviors just like Jesus Christ as we stand beside Him in victory.

If you have never asked anyone if they want to know Jesus, I want to share with you bits of wisdom I was blessed with by others. Stand strong in your faith, as this is very simple to do, and you will bring others to Jesus Christ because of His word living inside of you.

There is nothing on earth that gives you the feeling of pleasing God but the fulfillment of the most important thing to Him in His kingdom. If you are a soul champion, you are always trying to reach someone to bring to Christ and show them the way to eternal life.

This can basically work with anyone that you are speaking to, and it goes something like this:

"I have a question to ask you, and your opinion is very important to me."

"Okay…"

"If you died today, are you sure you would go to heaven?"

"I don't know."

"Let me tell you how you will absolutely know. Have you ever met Jesus Christ?"

This is just an example that works in person or just a conversation and is a great starting place to enter into the subject of Jesus Christ that no person should ever miss out on, which is eternal life and passing death to be in the kingdom of heaven forever with the Father and the Son. Remember to find the version of you that God has created in you so you can reach out and save others through His Word, as He saved you.

Now we have come to the final thought of this message: by knowing God's love for us, we know how to love others, and that motivates us to share the love of God with them so that they can experience God's fullness. Once we see how precious all people are to God, we will do all we can to win them to Christ. Humanity needs a Savior, for humans cannot save themselves.

You have a soul that is of greater value than the whole world. One of two things will happen to your soul: your soul will be saved, or your soul will be lost. I want your soul to be saved. I want to walk the streets of heaven with you and praise our Lord. Will you join me?

One of the most important commitments you can make as a Christian is to read your Bible every day. In each message, we will provide you with a few scriptures to look up and read on your own

to plant seeds inside of you for a deeper understanding so you can grow closer to Jesus Christ through His written word.

It's time to get your Bible. For your growing with God, scriptures for "The Number One Way to Please God" are Hebrews 11:6, Proverbs 16:7, and Colossians 1:10.

I pray that this message creates a path for you to grow closer to Jesus Christ or meet Him for the first time. If you want to receive the guaranteed passage that He sacrificed Himself on the cross for so you can be saved as a child of God, then become who you are created to be and turn the words you read in this book into action now so you can have eternal life in the kingdom of heaven that is just waiting for you.

Planting Notes:

_____

_____

_____

_____

_____

Is Your GPS Turned On?
(God's Positioning System)

We have become a society that seems unable to find its way anywhere without some type of device leading us around as if we have no sense to find our own direction or make our own decisions. A device telling us where to go, what to do, and how to act. Unfortunately, all of these devices keep you lost if you don't have the GPS God placed in you turned on.

Let me ask you something: Are you not sure what direction you are going in life? Is your GPS turned on? Your *GPS*? What? Yes, your GPS, your God's Positioning System that all of us have as children of God, which will always have the right direction for us to go in to be all God intends us to be.

Most of us have used a GPS to help us get where we want to go in life so that we don't get lost. We even count on our GPS to redirect us to get us back on track in the right direction. To be completely honest: when people's GPS isn't working, it sends most of them straight into a panic and the feeling of being lost and that they won't be able to find where they need to be or are going. Does any of this sound familiar? So, if you trust a computer device to lead you around in life, believing it will take you where you want to go, have you placed the same faith in your own internal GPS that God gave you?

Well, then what have you done for your own life to make sure your life goes in the right direction? If you go, of course, you will be redirected back on the right path you are intended to be on, so your directions are so clear that if you follow them exactly, you will never get lost again.

That is exactly what God does for you, for your life, with His Word. Everything has already been preprogrammed for you to avoid anything in life that would cause you to be lost, and it never has to be updated. No matter where you are in the entire world, these directions will get you where you need to be according to God's Word.

With a GPS, if you go off the directions that it is taking you, then you will definitely get lost and possibly create total destruction until you redirect your GPS or start following the instructions it is telling you to do to guarantee you get yourself going in the right direction.

Just like with correction, you may have a season where you feel lost and confused about where you are. Why are you here? And how do you get out of here? God may want change in us or to get us back on the right path of our salvation as His children because we have wandered away from His directions and are becoming lost, and God works just like your car GPS does. He redirects you automatically through His Word.

Just like the GPS in your car or on your phone, with God's Positioning System, you have the choice to follow these directions in order to guarantee you get where you need to be in life. If you choose to take shortcuts or wander somewhere you are not supposed to be, you may be exposed to consequences for taking that shortcut that may take you even longer to get where you need to be in life if you ever do. Jesus never took a shortcut on anything in His existence.

Let's visit some clear directions God gives us in a couple of scriptures so we can have a better understanding that our GPS, God's Positioning System, is in us from birth, and it will always be at work, keeping you from getting lost and on the right direction as a child of God.

Let us visit the scripture of Isaiah 55:9: "For as the heavens are higher than the earth, so are my ways higher than your ways and my thoughts than your thoughts."

"I will instruct you and teach you in the way you should go; I will counsel you with my eye upon you" (Psalm 32:8).

"The steps of a man are established by the LORD, when he delights in his way; though he fall, he shall not be cast headlong, for the LORD upholds his hand" (Psalm 37:23–24).

Next, we will visit the scripture of Proverbs 3:5–6: "Trust in the LORD with all your heart, and do not lean on your own understanding. In all your ways acknowledge him, and he will make straight your paths."

One of the most important commitments you can make as a Christian is to read your Bible every day. In each message, we will provide you with a few scriptures to look up and read on your own to plant seeds inside of you for a deeper understanding so you can grow closer to Jesus Christ through His written word.

It's time to get your Bible. For your growing with God, scriptures for "Is Your GPS Turned On?" are Jeremiah 29:11, Proverbs 3:5–6, and Psalm 37:23–24.

I pray that this message creates a path for you to grow closer to Jesus Christ or meet Him for the first time. If you want to receive the guaranteed passage that He sacrificed Himself on the cross for so you can be saved as a child of God, then become who you are created to be and turn the words you read in this book into action now so you can have eternal life in the kingdom of heaven that is just waiting for you.

Planting Notes:

_____

_____

_____

_____

_____

Faith: a Map to Jesus

Would you follow a map if it guaranteed all the riches you could dream of would be there? Of course, you would because it is a guaranteed direction to reach your location and desires. Faith works in exactly the same way and is the only map you need to find salvation in Jesus Christ, guaranteeing you will never be lost.

Let's look at what the blessings are inside the word "faith." Faith is the must-have ingredient to begin a relationship with God. Faith is the assurance that the things revealed and promised in the Word are true, even though unseen, and it gives the believer a conviction and peace that what he or she expects by having faith will come to pass.

What is faith according to God's Word? Let's explore Hebrews 11:1: "Now faith is the assurance of things hoped for, the conviction of things not seen." The evidence of your conviction, belief, and living the life of God's Word is so positive and powerful that it is described as faith.

You may ask yourself, "What is the purpose of faith?" The purpose of faith is to believe in oneself and allow God to come into your life and take control. Faith becomes an undeniable truth and is essential to your belief as a child of God and a Christian.

Now, let's look at what the word "faith" can mean in your life:

F – Forgiven

Let's start with the scripture of 1 John 1:9: "If we confess our sins, he is faithful and just to forgive us our sins and to cleanse us from all unrighteousness."

Your very first step to faith is to ask for forgiveness of your sins so God can forgive you of all of your sins. This is the first step to acquiring faith. You must break the chains of sin and leave them in God's hands to be saved and born again.

A – Assurance

Our next scripture is Philippians 4:6–7:

> Do not be anxious about anything, but in everything by prayer and supplication with thanksgiving let your requests be made known to God. And the peace of God, which surpasses all understanding, will guard your hearts and your minds in Christ Jesus.

The next part of faith is you have to accept God's forgiveness and understand you are born new again. You must believe you have been forgiven, as His Word says you have. You are to leave the ways of the world behind you and seek Him as if He was the air you breathe through His Word and prayer.

You need to know and believe that, no matter what season God has you in, you are to be thankful to be His child and that He always has the best for your life even if you do not understand. You must let the peace and joy of God saturate your heart and spirit and walk in His lighted path.

By accepting God as your Lord and Savior, you will be protected by Him as His child through your commitment to His Word, the Father, the Son, and the Holy Spirit.

I – I AM

Our next scripture is Revelation 1:8: "'I am the Alpha and the Omega,' says the Lord God, 'who is and who was and who is to come, the Almighty.'"

You must, with all your heart, mind, and soul, believe and know that God is real and that He was here in the beginning, long before you were born as His miracle, during your life with you in this world, and that God will be in heaven waiting on you as His child coming home.

You must know that there is only one real God who can forgive you of all of your sins and save you for eternal life with the Father and the Son in the kingdom of heaven.

T – Truth

Now we are going to the scripture of John 14:6: "Jesus said to him, 'I am the way, and the truth, and the life. No one comes to the Father except through me.'"

This is where you must understand that God's way is the only way you were created to exist and that all else is forms of evil, trying to destroy what God has created. Listen: don't miss this. God is truth, and the truth is with all He says, and He cannot and does not lie, deceive, or betray. Your only way to salvation and eternal life as His child is through His Word and His Son, Jesus Christ, so you become who He intends you to be as His child.

H – Heaven

Let's review God's Word about heaven with the scripture of John 14:2: "In my Father's house are many rooms. If it were not so, would I have told you that I go to prepare a place for you?"

This is your cornerstone; this is your rock that you now are fully aware of and have a complete understanding of: faith is the map to Jesus Christ with salvation, eternal life, and all the blessings that come with being a child of God as you were intended to be, including that you have to be keeping your faith always.

You now absolutely know the destination God has for you in your life as His child and that faith is your guaranteed map to Jesus Christ. Without faith, it is also impossible to please God and follow His Word. This is so important: God is once again telling you He has already made a place for you in heaven because His Son saved you. Do not doubt the Word of God, as He is the truth and you are to rely on the Father for everything as His child through your faith.

Let's discuss a few ways to keep your faith looking up, even when life brings you seasons of challenges.

1. Get the ball rolling first thing every morning: get in your prayer space, read the Word of God, and pray for His guidance, protection, and love in your life to glorify His name as His child.
2. Pray. Ask God for the strength to love the Father, the Son, and others in the way He loves you and has intended you to love.
3. Find a way to bless others to keep your focus on being a servant of God and not on what God will take care of for you if you lay it down to the Father.
4. Get inspired, motivated, and continually read and expose yourself to the Word of God.
5. Surround yourself with spiritual leaders and other believers that can help you grow your faith.

One of the most important commitments you can make as a Christian is to read your Bible every day. In each message, we will provide you with a few scriptures to look up and read on your own to plant seeds inside of you for a deeper understanding so you can grow closer to Jesus Christ through His written word.

It's time to get your Bible. For your growing with God, scriptures for "Faith: a Map to Jesus" are Romans 10:17, Mark 11:22–24, and Luke 1:37.

I pray that this message creates a path for you to grow closer to Jesus Christ or meet Him for the first time. If you want to receive the guaranteed passage that He sacrificed Himself on the cross for so you can be saved as a child of God, then become who you are created to be and turn the words you read in this book into action now so you can have eternal life in the kingdom of heaven that is just waiting for you.

Planting Notes:

_____

_____

_____

_____

_____

HOPE

What is the real meaning of hope? What do you hope for? Is hope a good or a bad emotion? Does hope even matter, or should it matter? Hope gives you strength from God. Without hope, you can never have joy, patience, and peace, as hope is a key ingredient for you to receive the power of the Holy Spirit within you.

As Jesus walked the earth, He carried a message of hope to everyone. But do you really know what hope truly means? Do you know it means to put everyone else in front of yourself? It means putting others' needs before your own at any cost. Is it how you live your life? Do you know that Jesus lived every moment of His life, putting everyone else's needs in front of His own, and died on the cross doing that?

Do you know the action of putting others before you brings you closer to God? Do you feel Jesus shine brightly inside of you with joy and love when you care for others? Do you feel fulfilled by loving others? Do you want to follow in the same footsteps as Jesus? Do you want to be the Christian you are intended to be as a child of God?

When you put others before yourself, you are doing exactly what God expects of you. There is no greater action to put others in front of you than dying on the cross. That brings us to what the true message of hope is in Christ. The purpose of Jesus is based on the word "hope." Helping Other People Every Day, H.O.P.E., is what Jesus does with all that have or will ever meet Him.

There is a love that occurs in you when you do something for others. It is amazing: when love becomes a strong part of God in you, you do things for others, and they never know who did it. You give all glory to the Lord and Savior for allowing you to bless others through Him.

Every day, when you wake, your first thought should be, *How can I serve you today, Lord?* Then you begin by putting others in front of you and letting God bless you for your obedience. Remember putting someone in front of you doesn't require you to do big things, as small actions make big changes when done for the love of serving others.

Let's see what the scriptures say about putting others' needs in front of your own. We will begin with 1 John 3:17: "But if anyone has the world's goods and sees his brother in need, yet closes his heart against him, how does God's love abide in him?" In this scripture, you must learn that if you are given the wealth of the world and turn on your brother or sister in need and ignore them, you will be sinning against God.

How do you expect God to know who you are? How do you know who God is, as His children do not behave in this manner? Make sure that, if you are given the wealth of the world, you put others in front of you and allow that blessing to be shared by others through your love of them because your wealth only comes from God, who has already provided you with an entire kingdom.

Now, let's explore our next scripture, Proverbs 19:17: "Whoever is generous to the poor lends to the LORD, and he will repay him for his deed." This is where your faith and belief that God provides for His children are put to the test. You must acknowledge that all you have and all you will ever be is because the Lord will watch over you as His child.

If you have no food and $2 to your name in church or you find someone in need, you tithe the $2 and trust the Lord or give that person in need your last two dollars and introduce them to Jesus. Tell them they are loved and wanted and He is waiting on them to come home. You can show them the way if they want to meet Him.

We will conclude our scriptures in this message with Luke 12:33–34:

> Sell your possessions, and give to the needy. Provide yourselves with moneybags that do not grow old, with a treasure in the heavens that does not fail, where no thief approaches and no moth destroys. For where your treasure is, there will your heart be also.

What an amazing verse that teaches us there is no amount of wealth in the world that can compare to the riches of God that will never end, can never be taken from you, and can never be destroyed. Your relationship with Him is priceless as a father's to his child would be.

Just as He always puts you first, then you must do this with others to show them they can have what you do and it all comes from loving one another and placing others before you always as Christ has all of us. When you have done this, you will then understand and know the true meaning of H.O.P.E., Helping Other People Every Day.

One of the most important commitments you can make as a Christian is to read your Bible every day. In each message, we will provide you with a few scriptures to look up and read on your own to plant seeds inside of you for a deeper understanding so you can grow closer to Jesus Christ through His written word.

It's time to get your Bible. For your growing with God, scriptures for the message "Hope" are Isaiah 58:20, Proverbs 22:9, 1 John 4:11, and Philippians 2:4.

I pray that this message creates a path for you to grow closer to Jesus Christ or meet Him for the first time. If you want to receive the guaranteed passage that He sacrificed Himself on the cross for so you can be saved as a child of God, then become who you are created to be and turn the words you read in this book into action now so you can have eternal life in the kingdom of heaven that is just waiting for you.

Planting Notes:

_____

_____

_____

_____

_____

WALLS

Have you ever felt closed in with no way out? Desperate and lost with no answers? Do you know that if there is anything you have not laid down to God, He will not be able to hear you or even know you? Do you create your own roadblocks in life? Do you know that any wall you have can cause blindness because you can't see through walls, only knock them down and get rid of them?

Have you ever been surrounded by walls and believed you couldn't escape? Walls are meant to keep things out but also to protect things as well. Do you think walls are just physical objects? Have you heard someone say, "I climbed over that wall," or "It was too big to get over the wall"? Sometimes people try to go around walls that are in their way, but usually, shortcuts do not work; they just tend to make the wall bigger.

Do you have any walls that are blocking you from your relationship and blessings with God? Are you willing to admit you have walls that are preventing you from being who God intends you to be? Did you know walls can be almost anything that stops us from being what we are supposed to be as children of God?

It could be a painful event from a childhood that you can't let go of as an adult; you could have done something that you have never shared with anyone; pride, jealousy, divorce, guilt, money, or maybe the ways of the world are all walls blocking everything God has intended for you.

Do you know there is no wall too big that God can't help you get over? Do you know if you have walls up, you are blocking everything from yourself, including your relationship with God? You can't hear or see through walls, so how does anyone know you are even there?

Walls destroy everything, as they are borders around the heart, mind, and soul that block you from what God has intended for you to become. They destroy you from the inside out. But overcoming walls brings you closer to God. God is here to handle everything, including any wall you have in your life that prevents you from being with Him.

If you are not overcoming your walls through Christ, then you have allowed your faith to waiver. Now, walls may also be there for many reasons, as God allows everything to happen for a reason or a season.

Keep in mind: a wall is not getting something you want that God does not agree with, as you can easily run into the wall of impatience and have to spend a season learning patience when those events occur in your life. Do not create walls in your life that are not supposed to be there.

Remember: God does everything in His perfect timing and what is best for you. But if you have walls up and in the way, then you may have just put your life in a maze and become lost.

What should you do with the walls in your life? Give them to God, lay them down, and ask Him to remove them from you. Give up your self-control and trying to fix what only God can change. So, let's look at scriptures on why you should not have walls in your life.

Let's start with the scripture in 2 Corinthians 10:5 (KJV): "Casting down imaginations, and every high thing that exalteth itself against the knowledge of God, and bringing into captivity every thought to the obedience of Christ."

The life God has in store for you comes from being both fully present and then fully loved by the Father. You can't experience the love of God and others if you don't allow yourself to be present. In order to be present, there must be nothing between you and what you are present for, which is God. You can only be present by being one-on-one with God.

We can't experience God's grace and affection for us if we build walls around ourselves from Him. You must lay down all your walls in life to God. He will never reject you, as no wall is too big, so have no fear.

Walls prevent you from receiving and giving real, true love that comes from God only. If you live with walls up around you, it isn't really living; it's surviving. You are suffering when peace is waiting for you. God knows your pains and your wounds. He knows how to heal you.

The scripture of Psalm 34:18 says, "The LORD is near to the brokenhearted and saves the crushed in spirit." God is for you. God is your biggest cheerleader because you are His child. He longs to be near to you and save you for eternal life with Him in the kingdom of heaven.

But in order for you to experience the fullness of His love and healing, you have to let Him in. You have to be fully present to God, which means all your walls must be laid down, let go, and you have to let Him take care of them. In order for you to experience true life, you have to stop struggling with your walls and start trusting in the powerful, capable hands of your loving Father that has your best interest always.

Now we will explore the scripture of Psalm 57:7 (NLT), where David writes, "My heart is confident in you, O God; my heart is confident." God is the one who protects our hearts. There is nothing we can do to fully protect ourselves from the wars of the world around us except allow our hearts to be fully open to God. Only in God can we trust. And only in God will we experience a true, full eternal life as His child.

As a final thought: please take time every day to tear down and bury your walls, no matter what they are. Stop placing your hope in the ways of the world and waiting for things to get better. You must only look to God as your great protector who will not allow walls to imprison you as long as you are fully present to Him. Spend your time in deep prayer and laying those walls down to God to eliminate what threatens you as His child and receive His love, freedom, and deliverance in the Holy Spirit with eternal life.

One of the most important commitments you can make as a Christian is to read your Bible every day. In each message, we will provide you with a few scriptures to look up and read on your own to plant seeds inside of you for a deeper understanding so you can grow closer to Jesus Christ through His written word.

It's time to get your Bible. For your growing with God, scriptures for the message "Walls" are Psalm 122:7, Joshua 6:20, and Psalm 119:11.

I pray that this message creates a path for you to grow closer to Jesus Christ or meet Him for the first time. If you want to receive the guaranteed passage that He sacrificed Himself on the cross for so you can be saved as a child of God, then become who you are created to be and turn the words you read in this book into action now so you can have eternal life in the kingdom of heaven that is just waiting for you.

Planting Notes:

_____

_____

_____

_____

_____

Why Does God Love You So Much?

How important is it to be loved? Does it matter who loves you or why they love you? Can you love God if you don't love yourself? Can God love you if you don't love yourself? Do you love others as you want to be loved? Why is love so important? Because without love, there can be no relationship with God for your salvation.

First, we must understand that all children belong to God because of His creation in the beginning and that He loves all of us, as we are all His children. He is the Father of all who are the fruit of His creation and are His reward.

Let's come to an understanding that God first created the heavens and the earth and all that live on it. He created Adam and Eve and allowed Eve to have free will where she failed with one bite of an apple due to temptation by the serpent in the garden, and then, *bam*, sin was born instantly and covered the world.

Listen: this is an amazing example of God's awesome power. It only took Eve one bite of an apple, and the reaction by God was so powerful it didn't take a day, a week, or even a year for the plague of evil and sin to consume the entire world. It was instant: in the very second that bite of the apple occurred, immediately, sin and evil were born and now are loose on the world, open for the business of destroying your salvation as a child of God.

So, remember: when you commit sin, it is the instant destruction of you as a child of God and God's reaction can be immediate or come in lessons, according to what He feels is best for you as His child.

There is nothing more powerful than God's Word and the correction that comes from not following it as you were clearly instructed to as His child. God allowed the world to be saturated in sin because Eve did not follow His word, and sin was the correction for her and all attached to her for eternity, and that includes all of us.

As God observed His child (the world) growing, He became ever more aware of the potential destruction of His creation by evil. That brings us to John 3:16: "For God so loved the world, that he gave his only Son, that whoever believes in him should not perish but have eternal life." There is nothing more that God can do to prove how much He loves all of us, including you, than sacrificing His Son for your salvation.

Now let us visit 1 John 3:1: "See what kind of love the Father has given to us, that we should be called children of God; and so we are. The reason why the world does not know us is that it did not know him."

God knew He had to create a way to save His creation (us as His children), and that is exactly what He did with the birth, sacrifice, death, and resurrection of His only Son, Jesus. He created a path directly for all of us to be saved and washed clean of sin and reborn again, for those who believe in His Son and follow His Word will be given eternal life in the kingdom of heaven as children of God.

This path also separates us from the ways of the world and is the only path to righteousness in the kingdom of heaven. Those that follow the ways of the world are of sin and evil because they do not know the Father nor the Son, and all who follow the path of the world are certain to perish for eternity with the devil.

Now we know how much God loves us because He sacrificed His Only son for us. But why does God love us so much?

Let's begin with Psalm 127:3: "Behold, children are a heritage from the LORD, the fruit of the womb, a reward." This scripture is talking about why God loves you so much: as His creation, you are a miracle, His child, whom you become at birth to Him. As a new child, be prepared to experience the most exciting moment of your life, something remarkable (the birth of you as a child of God), and receive the most important reward for His kingdom.

Never believe God does not love you, no matter who you are or what you have done. We are all His children, and He is our Father, and we are all brothers and sisters, and His love for us is without end because we are His creation made in His image and will be for eternity.

One of the most important commitments you can make as a Christian is to read your Bible every day. In each message, we will provide you with a few scriptures to look up and read on your own to plant seeds inside of you for a deeper understanding so you can grow closer to Jesus Christ through His written word.

It's time to get your Bible. For your growing with God, scriptures for the message "Why Does God Love You So Much?" are Isaiah 41:10, John 15:13, and Psalm 86:15.

I pray that this message creates a path for you to grow closer to Jesus Christ or meet Him for the first time. If you want to receive the guaranteed passage that He sacrificed Himself on the cross for so you can be saved as a child of God, then become who you are created to be and turn the words you read in this book into action now so you can have eternal life in the kingdom of heaven that is just waiting for you.

Planting Notes:

_____

_____

_____

_____

_____

One Love

The word "love" is used in so many ways: "I love this," "I love that," and "I love you." How do you know what real love is? Are you feeling infatuation or love? The word and the meaning of what love is can be different for every person. When in actuality, there is only one true love through Christ and to love everything as Jesus loves, as we are made in His image.

Let's start with what God says love is in 1 Corinthians 13:4–5 (NIV):

> Love is patient, love is kind. It does not envy, it does not boast, it is not proud. It does not dishonor others, it is not self-seeking, it is not easily angered, and it keeps no record of wrongs.

Love is probably one of the most overused words in the world. It is used in so many different ways, such as "puppy love," "love of the body," "affectionate love," "people who love children," "love of food," "the love of material things," "playful love," "teenage love," "long-lasting love," "marital love," and many more.

But the reality is every kind of what we perceive love is, except for one, always comes down to that it is usually an infatuation of an object or person, which can appear as idolatry in many forms. Any type of love other than the love God has for you is an imitation of what love really is.

The love you have for God and the love you have for others should be exactly as God loves you. Loving God through loving the Son is the only real love that exists in the entire world. All types of love are usually fascination or fixation with a false identity and simply are not real and are not based on the one and only love that comes from knowing God as His child.

You must love everyone to the same decree that Jesus loved us and gave His life for our salvation and eternal life with the Father in the kingdom of heaven. You love your wife, your children, your extended family, your friends, your fellow believers, but unless you love God first and love them through His love for you, then it is not real love.

Anything else is a perception of what the world wants you to believe love is, so you will never have a clear understanding of what real love is by never knowing your Father in heaven and the Son. Therefore, it is robbing you of salvation and eternal life in the kingdom of heaven.

In order to experience real love, you must love everyone through God, with the same passion as He loves you, as true love has been displayed by the Father sacrificing His only Son and the Son sacrificing Himself to show how much you are loved that He was crucified to save you for eternity. Let's reveal God's word about love in Scripture with 1 John 4:7: "Beloved, let us love one another, for love is from God, and whoever loves has been born of God and knows God."

As you can see, God's Word is very clear that we should love one another and that love is only from God and that those that love others through God as His children are known by Him. The world cannot offer what it does not know, as it will have only distractions of deception to take what real love is away from you.

We will continue our scriptures with John 13:34: "A new commandment I give to you, that you love one another: just as I have loved you, you also are to love one another."

This is where God's word about love has been raised to the highest level of His word: that you are to consider His words about what love is and how you are supposed to love as a new commandment. Listen closely: God expects you to carry the same reverence in regard to His word about love as He expects from you in regard to the Ten Commandments. He has instructed you to specifically follow the to-be-considered base principles of His word for your life as His child so that He can be with you in the kingdom of heaven.

We will conclude this message with the scripture of 1 Peter 4:8: "Above all, keep loving one another earnestly, since love covers a multitude of sins."

This is incredible! Do you understand what this message is saying about how powerful God has made love through Him? If you follow His commandment and love in the way He has instructed, your sins can be covered. Love is so powerful God allows it to wash away your sins as if they vanish.

This is because you know God and understand that there is only one real love in existence. That *love* only comes through loving everyone through the Son and the Father and is the only way to experience, understand, and share with others what real love is. Otherwise, you may never know what real love is, but God has given you a guaranteed way to know what real love is. The choice is yours; He is always waiting.

One of the most important commitments you can make as a Christian is to read your Bible every day. In each message, we will provide you with a few scriptures to look up and read on your own to plant seeds inside of you for a deeper understanding so you can grow closer to Jesus Christ through His written word.

It's time to get your Bible. For your growing with God, scriptures for the message "One Love" are Romans 5:8, Zephaniah 3:17, and Ephesians 2:4–5.

I pray that this message creates a path for you to grow closer to Jesus Christ or meet Him for the first time. If you want to receive the guaranteed passage that He sacrificed Himself on the cross for so you can be saved as a child of God, then become who you are created to be and turn the words you read in this book into action now so you can have eternal life in the kingdom of heaven that is just waiting for you.

Planting Notes:

_____

_____

_____

_____

_____

Are You a Gambler?

Do you like to play games of chance and take all kinds of risks in the name of winning? What is the greatest prize you could ever desire to win? How many things do you do in life that are gambling with your relationship with God? If you knew you could have the greatest reward in your life you could ever win, would you do anything to be in that opportunity where you were a guaranteed winner?

First, let's start off with the fact we all know—that gambling is a sin. But the question is: Are you gambling every day and don't even know it, or are you fully aware and choose to gamble every day? The amazing thing is this kind of gambling doesn't even cost you one penny. The only thing you lose when you are gambling in this game is your eternal life and salvation, ending in death.

Yet, millions of people walk around every day and tip their toes in the water with Jesus and keep on going once they get a drink, then just keep going through the world, and do not realize that the more you know about Jesus, the more He is aware of you gambling with your salvation if you are playing with sin.

You need to submit yourself all unto the Father, His Word and direction for you to become a guaranteed winner with eternal life. So many people gamble with their relationship with God every day. They do not realize that not coming to church or just occasionally reading the Bible, only at church, and usually just what the sermon is about, and following the ways of the world can make them think they can walk that fine line that does not exist between sin and salvation. And that makes them guaranteed losers.

If this is what you do, then you are a gambler and betting on the most important things you will ever have, and that is your salvation and eternal life as a child of God in the kingdom with the Father and the Son. How do you think God is going to feel about your games of chance, putting you, His child, at risk after He lost His Son to save you?

Do not believe for one second, not even a minute, that everything you do, if it is not following the Word of God and living that way, does not determine whether you are a gambler or not. It does, and let's remind you that gambling is a sin in any form.

Now let's explore the Scriptures in regard to gambling. It is not only important that you read the Bible, but you must understand what the Bible is clearly saying to you. This allows your heart and mind to grow in understanding and be closer to Jesus Christ to become who God intended you to be as His child.

First, we will begin with a scripture from 1 Timothy 6:9–10:

> But those who desire to be rich fall into temptation,
> into a snare, into many senseless and harmful desires
> that plunge people into ruin and destruction [...]
> It is through this ungodly craving that some have
> wandered away from the faith and pierced themselves
> with many pangs.

This verse clearly spells out that there is gambling with sin and your salvation that takes place when you behave in this manner, and once you are caught in the traps of sin, it devours you. God is saying that any way that does not comply with His Word and what is expected of you as His child only has one direction and devastating result it will end with: It is the ruin and destruction of your salvation and eternal life. You can not only avoid participating in behaviors considered to be of a sinful nature and gambling with your salvation but also are not supposed to even think about them, as they only have one direction: they will lead you through a life of pain, ending in death, and take you up for a permanent residence with Satan.

Let's continue with a scripture from Luke 16:13: "No servant can serve two masters, for either he will hate the one and love the other, or he will be devoted to the one and despise the other."

Here we go: now you are playing heads or tails with your salvation. Being a child of God is not a fifty-fifty relationship with Jesus Christ because if you know Him and if you continue following the ways of sin and the world instead of His instructed word plainly written for you, you will certainly experience His correction and constant redirection to try and get you where you are supposed to be. God will cause you to make a choice, and gambling is a sin to Him, and that is what you are doing with your salvation in His eyes.

God wants His house to always win your soul, win your heart, and win your love. God is the only guaranteed winner in life that you should always bet on, as there is no other thing in existence that does what God does and covers your life in eternal blessings that a child of God receives by following the Word of the Father.

You are designed to be forgiven and saved as His child and to spend your eternal life that you were created for as His miracle with the Father and the Son in the kingdom of heaven.

We will conclude our scriptures on gambling with your salvation with Romans 12:2 (NIV): "Do not conform to the pattern of this world, but be transformed by the renewing of your mind."

Tell me, did you catch it? Did you hear the key to eliminating the risk of gambling with your salvation ever to occur? The key to eliminating the occurrence of gambling ever happening in your life is being transformed by the renewing of your mind with the Word of God. What does that exactly mean?

Well, listen: the mind can lead the heart, and the heart can lead the mind. The key is to have them work together, and that only occurs by the renewing of the body, mind, and spirit. We all get drained from being in this world as His children and run on spiritually empty and need God to fill us up and renew us by us praying, fellowshipping, and spending one-on-one time with Him.

Remember: you are what you see, read, and do, so all of these environments must be focused on living by the Word of God.

Otherwise, you have become a gambler and are putting your salvation at risk of discipline, correction, devastation, destruction, and ultimately, you will not pass death by but participate in it.

By constantly filling yourself back up with God's never-ending love and grace, gambling with your salvation will never happen. Surround yourself with other believers, attend church and spiritual events, put others before yourself always, read your Bible, speak the Word of God to others, pray, have a relationship with your Lord and Savior, and love everyone as God loves you. There is no need for gambling when you a part of a house that always wins.

So, we have learned that if you play with sin, you are a gambler, and that leads to more sin, and ultimately, the death of a child, your death as God's child, as you gambled away your own salvation in sin.

Always remember: gambling with a child of God's salvation is equal to an opportunity to accept the invitation to pass by your eternal life with the Father and the Son in the kingdom of heaven.

Not only does gambling with your salvation lead to deeper and deeper covetousness of sin, but it leads to different types of sin. So, you must always watch out for what you think about, say, and do, what environments you expose yourself to, think ahead, and act in the way God would expect of you as His child and according to His instructed word He has given you for the path of your life.

One of the most important commitments you can make as a Christian is to read your Bible every day. In each message, we will provide you with a few scriptures to look up and read on your own to plant seeds inside of you for a deeper understanding so you can grow closer to Jesus Christ through His written word.

It's time to get your Bible. For your growing with God, scriptures for the message "Are You a Gambler?" are Timothy 6:10, Luke 12:15, and Proverbs 28:22.

I pray that this message creates a path for you to grow closer to Jesus Christ or meet Him for the first time. If you want to receive the guaranteed passage that He sacrificed Himself on the cross for so you can be saved as a child of God, then become who you are created to be and turn the words you read in this book into action now so you can have eternal life in the kingdom of heaven that is just waiting for you.

Planting Notes:

_____

_____

_____

_____

_____

You Can't Serve Two Masters

Are you made in the image of Adam or Jesus? Do you follow the ways of the world and go to church on Sunday? Do you cuss with one breath and pray in the next? Do you sin and ask for forgiveness and then do the sin again? Do you know if you are saved or just think you might be? Is everything in your life consumed by confusion or calmness?

In this message, we are going to explore the Word in regard to what will happen if you try to serve two masters so that we have a deeper understanding of God's Word. What does "serving two masters" mean? What does serving two masters do to me? Why do I need to know what God says about serving two masters?

The first thing that you must realize: in the world we live in, you are born into sin automatically; that puts you in a position of choice. How will you live your life as a miracle from God? Will you be lost in the ways of the world and forgotten? Do you think you can walk that fine line between faith and failure? Why did I say "failure"? We all know that faith in Jesus Christ will lead us to eternal life, and the other option in how you dedicate your only life is failure that ends in your death.

You cannot go in two different ways at the same time on a street. Have you ever noticed there are one-way streets, and if you go in the wrong direction, you could end in serious trouble, even death? So why do you think you can keep going back and forth in between the direction of God and Satan and get away with it? Whether you realize it or not, you have set your soul up for war on a daily basis for your entire life that will pass eternal life by and end in death.

Do you want to live in war and strife your entire life, ending in death, or peace and eternal life in the kingdom of heaven? The choice is yours, as you are not guaranteed a ticket to heaven just because you were born. Now, we are going to explore God's Word in regard to trying to serve two masters with your soul.

We will begin with the scripture of Matthew 6:24: "No one can serve two masters, for either he will hate the one and love the other, or he will be devoted to the one and despise the other. You cannot serve God and money."

In this scripture, God is clearly telling you what will happen if you try to serve two masters. You will be filled with hate, turmoil, and conflict, causing your soul to be put at risk of never seeing eternal life and the kingdom of heaven. You cannot dip your toe into the fire and not get burned. Think about this, as most have experienced it.

How do you feel when you get a burn on you, even just a small one? It is so painful immediately, and it does not care who you are. You can be a child or adult, as Satan is not picky; he just wants your soul. Could you even imagine allowing your whole body to get scorched by Satan forever? That is a little preview of the pain you could suffer in hell.

Next are words from the scripture of Joshua 24:15: "And if it is evil in your eyes to serve the LORD, choose this day whom you will serve [...] But as for me and my house, we will serve the LORD."

Jesus spoke these words as part of His Sermon on the Mount in which He had said it was foolish to store up "treasures on earth, where moths and vermin destroy, and where thieves break in and steal" (Matthew 6:19, NIV).

> Do not lay up for yourselves treasures on earth, where moth and rust destroy and where thieves break in and steal, but lay up for yourselves treasures in heaven, where neither moth nor rust destroys and where thieves do not break in and steal.

Matthew 6:19–20

He urged us to store up treasure in heaven, where it will last forever.

The obstacle that prevents us from wise investment is the heart. "For where your treasure is, there your heart will be also" (Matthew 6:21). We follow what has captivated our hearts, and Jesus made it clear that we cannot serve two masters.

Do you understand a master is anything that enslaves us, as in Romans 6:16?

> Do you not know that if you present yourselves to anyone as obedient slaves, you are slaves of the one whom you obey, either of sin, which leads to death, or of obedience, which leads to righteousness?

Alcohol, lust, and money are all masters of some people. In a warning by Jesus that we cannot serve two masters, He specifies the love of money is a tool of Satan and is a master in opposition to God.

The Lord describes Himself as a "jealous God" in the scripture of Exodus 34:14: "For you shall worship no other god, for the LORD, whose name is Jealous, is a jealous God."

This means He guards what is rightfully His. He is righteously jealous of our affections because we were created to know and love Him. He is not jealous for His own sake; He needs nothing. He is jealous of us because we need Him. When we serve another master, we rob ourselves of all we were created for and God of His rightful adoration.

Jesus's claim to us is exclusive and belongs to no one else. He bought and paid the price for us with His own blood and delivered us from our former master, sin. He doesn't share His throne with anyone. During Jesus's time on the earth, some people followed Him for a time, but their devotion was superficial and fake. They wanted something Jesus offered, but they weren't committed to Him. The ways of the world were more important. They wanted to serve two masters, do you?

We cannot serve two masters because, as Jesus pointed out, we end up hating one and loving the other. It's only natural. Opposing masters demand different things and lead us down different paths. The Lord is headed in one direction, and our flesh and the world are headed in the other. A choice must be made. When we follow Christ, we must die to everything else, or we won't make it to the kingdom of heaven.

If we attempt to serve two masters, we will have divided loyalties, and when the difficulties of discipleship clash with the lure of fleshly pleasure, the magnetic pull of wealth and worldly success will draw you away from Christ and destroy every blessing intended for you.

Our call to godliness goes against the sinful nature we are born into. Only with the help of the Holy Spirit can we remain devoted to one Master. If you try to serve both God and sin, you will only end up serving sin, and God will lose sight of you, possibly forever.

Many pastors are watering down the gospel and twisting words of the Bible to make people happy because of their greed. Do you have an idol in your life? Maybe it's some sin, sports, hobbies, etc. God will not share His glory with anyone, or anything, who put anything before Him. Without Christ, you have nothing. He is the reason for your next breath.

The things in this world will not satisfy you. Everything in this world will disappear, but God will be forever. He will provide for you, but you must trust in Him alone. Stop compromising your soul because God doesn't share you with anyone, and the consequences of serving another master are pain, suffering, and ultimately death bypassing eternal life.

One of the most important commitments you can make as a Christian is to read your Bible every day. In each message, we will provide you with a few scriptures to look up and read on your own to plant seeds inside of you for a deeper understanding so you can grow closer to Jesus Christ through His written word.

It's time to get your Bible. For your growing with God, scriptures for the message "You Can't Serve Two Masters" are Luke 16:13–15, 1 Corinthians 10:21, and Deuteronomy 6:5.

I pray that this message creates a path for you to grow closer to Jesus Christ or meet Him for the first time. If you want to receive the guaranteed passage that He sacrificed Himself on the cross for so you can be saved as a child of God, then become who you are created to be and turn the words you read in this book into action now so you can have eternal life in the kingdom of heaven that is just waiting for you.

Planting Notes:

_____

_____

_____

_____

_____

YOUR REARVIEW MIRROR

Everyone has a rearview mirror in their car and the life that looks behind them. But why? It seems unnecessary when you are looking ahead and moving forward. When in reality, the rearview mirror is only there to protect you from making mistakes while you are moving forward, not to look backward to what you have left behind you.

Have you ever noticed how you constantly look in the rearview mirror behind you when you are going forward? Do you know many people miss what is in front of them, looking at what is behind them too much? Do you know when you are saved, you are blind to your past because who you were no longer exists?

If you focus on what is behind you, how will you ever see what is ahead of you? If all you see is that your past is your present, then how can God restore you and bless you? Do you constantly adjust your rearview mirror, trying to change what you see behind you? Do you look in your rearview mirror more than when you are in your car?

Do you realize there is a rearview mirror in your mind, heart, and soul? Do you realize that you have to release everything that was part of who you were in your mind, body, and soul forever? You must lay it down to God. Leaving your past to be born new again is leaving your entire past, as it is dead and you are now new in every way, without a past but with a future as a child of God. Nothing new or born new has a past.

What does God have to say about looking behind you, which is a dead end, instead of ahead of you, as you are born new again? Let's look at the scripture of Isaiah 43:18–19:

> Remember not the former things, nor consider the things of old. Behold, I am doing a new thing; now it springs forth, do you not perceive it? I will make a way in the wilderness and rivers in the desert.

How wonderful it is that God's Word has removed the past from our memory as long as we are looking forward to Him and what He has for us as His children! You are new again in every way, and you need to commit yourself to the way, the truth, and the life. It is often said you believe what you see. You must perceive, no matter what time has in store for you, God will take you through anything on the path for you to be with Him because He loves you so much and never gives up.

Let's visit another scripture about leaving your past behind you, Philippians 3:13–14:

> Brothers, I do not consider that I have made it my own. But one thing I do: forgetting what lies behind and straining forward to what lies ahead, I press on toward the goal for the prize of the upward call of God in Christ Jesus.

This scripture is where God wants your heart to be in His hands. You have become so strong in your faith with the Lord and Savior you announce it in who you are and what you do and know it is not of your own works. You are steadfast in forgetting your past, pressing forward into your relationship with God, and becoming who He intends you to be as His child.

One major problem about looking in your rearview mirror is the picture constantly changes and is never really in focus, exactly as you are when you are lost. Your future is not behind you; what is behind you is supposed to fade away into nonexistence when you are saved as His Word instructs you to be.

When you are looking forward and are with God, you can see everything clearly and can see what direction you are going in. You have a path He has prepared for you so that you will never be lost again. All you have to do is follow it through His word in the Bible and your faith.

Next, we will visit our last scripture in this message, Galatians 2:20:

> I have been crucified with Christ. It is no longer I who live, but Christ who lives in me. And the life I now live in the flesh I live by faith in the Son of God, who loved me and gave himself for me.

This scripture states that you clearly are saved and have allowed your sins to die on the cross with Jesus and be born again. You now know you are no longer who you were but who you are in Christ. You will only live your life according to His Word, by faith in Him, because of what He has done for you so you can be forgiven, saved, and born new again for eternal life in the kingdom with Him.

At some point in our lives, most of us stop living out of our imagination and start living out of memory. That's the day we stop living and start dying. To be fully alive is to be fully present, looking forward. And to do that, you've got to leave the past in the past.

God says, "For I will forgive their wickedness and will remember their sins no more" (Hebrews 8:12, NIV). Most people don't realize God uses an eraser all the time to wipe our past out of existence so we will be clean and new again. In Hebrews, God not only wipes our past sins away, but He forgives us of our sins and acts as if they never even happened once we become saved through Jesus Christ.

Our final thought in this message that you must understand is you won't find God in the past. His name is not "I was." His name is "I Am." If we obsess over what God did last, we'll miss what He wants to do next for us. God's at work right here, right now. God's always doing something new for all of His children for eternity. You cannot change your past; it is washed away for your eternal future in Christ.

One of the most important commitments you can make as a Christian is to read your Bible every day. In each message, we will provide you with a few scriptures to look up and read on your own

to plant seeds inside of you for a deeper understanding so you can grow closer to Jesus Christ through His written word.

It's time to get your Bible. For your growing with God, scriptures for the message "Your Rearview Mirror" are Acts 2:38, 2 Corinthians 5:17, and Luke 9:62.

I pray that this message creates a path for you to grow closer to Jesus Christ or meet Him for the first time. If you want to receive the guaranteed passage that He sacrificed Himself on the cross for so you can be saved as a child of God, then become who you are created to be and turn the words you read in this book into action now so you can have eternal life in the kingdom of heaven that is just waiting for you.

Planting Notes:

_____

_____

_____

_____

_____

Who Is Blessed by Forgiveness?

Forgiving someone can be one of the hardest things we do in our lives. Being hurt emotionally or physically can change us forever. Harboring ill feelings toward others or yourself honestly just makes you sick because it is not godly to behave in this manner. So, in reality, who is really blessed by forgiveness? You, the person you are forgiving, or both?

Do you know what forgiveness is? Do you forgive others? Do you want forgiveness from others? Do you want forgiveness from God? Do you feel that forgiving someone is giving them a blessing? Or is your forgiveness to them giving you a blessing? Do you know the answer?

How many things are even possible in your life when you get blessed as much as someone does from receiving the blessing of forgiveness from you? Does God forgive someone because you forgave them? Well, actually, yes, because forgiveness is from the heart of God, and you are instructed to forgive as He forgave you. So, when you forgive someone, you are forgiving them through the forgiveness of the heart of Christ inside of you.

It is providing the forgiveness that is most like Jesus and is a blessing from Him to you for doing as He would, as we are made in His image in every way. You always need to remember that you must accept forgiveness in order to be able to give forgiveness to someone else.

If you are unable to accept forgiveness, how can you be saved? If you never accept forgiveness, you are always living in the past. Why?

Because after you are saved, you already have accepted forgiveness and have buried the past at the cross behind you forever.

Now there is an understanding of why you follow God's Word. Because when you are born new again and forgiven, you can give forgiveness to others as Jesus Christ forgave you. Giving forgiveness is a blessing from you to others but is also a blessing from God for you, as He sees you following His Word as His child.

Though not the same as reconciliation or trust, forgiveness makes those at least possible if one is truly sorry for what they have done. Forgiveness can represent a lot of different things to many people. But in reality, there is only one type of forgiveness, and that is through Jesus Christ, who forgave you of all of your sins. Forgiveness turns sin into the blessing of eternal life.

For Christians, the greatest reason to forgive others is the forgiveness that God has already granted us. Ephesians 4:32 (KJV) says, "And be ye kind one to another, tenderhearted, forgiving one another, even as God for Christ's sake hath forgiven you."

Forgiving another person means not holding the offense over the offender's head and not having an attitude of hostility toward them. Committing sin after being saved does not take away a Christian's salvation or change their eternal standing before God, but it does hinder that person's relationship with God and how He relates to him or her.

Christians want to experience God's presence and have God's peace and guidance evident in their life; confessing sin, repenting, and asking God for forgiveness on a regular basis keeps their humble relationship with God where He expects them to be as His children.

Jesus said, "I tell you, not seven times, but seventy-seven times" (Matthew 18:22, NIV). "You, Lord, are forgiving and good, abounding in love to all who call to you" (Psalm 86:5, NIV). "And when you stand praying, if you hold anything against anyone, forgive them, so that your Father in heaven may forgive you your sins" (Mark 11:25, NIV).

Remember that God commands us to forgive, and He only commands the best for His people. The benefits of forgiveness include blessings, freedom, and better relationships. Forgiveness improves physical and mental health. It also starts us on the road to healing and living in the present through acting as Jesus Christ would.

The act of forgiveness is commanded from God, and every commandment from God is good, and it is wise to obey every command from God. The Bible says Christians must forgive (Colossians 3:13), and God will bless you when you forgive those who have sinned against you.

Forgiveness decreases resentment. Like water on a fire, forgiveness extinguishes bitterness and resentment by eliminating its fuel.

When you forgive someone, you do not excuse their actions, but you refuse to use their actions as a weapon against them. It involves an intentional decision not to fall into anger but to hand the resentment and the punishment over to God. This is how God demonstrates forgiveness of our sins. God handles the punishment, and God does not ponder on our sin. He washes it away and forgets it through forgiveness.

The act of forgiveness can bring peace. But resentment, which is the total opposite of peace, brings strife. Resentment decreases, and peace increases. If you are intentional to forgive, you will see God fill the void left by sin with peace, and this peace is far better than the hollow victory of "winning" any conflict with others in sin.

The act of forgiveness promotes love for God and others. Forgiveness increases our awareness of God's love by reminding us of Jesus's death for us. We are motivated to forgive when we remember God's forgiveness of our sins. This results in greater love for God and others and is what God commands us to do as His children.

The act of forgiveness increases awareness of our own sin. As your love for God grows inside of you, your first priority is to please God. Then the heart of forgiveness will grow in you as well. When you desire to please God, His love grows in you, then you become more aware of what pleases and displeases God. The result is that you desire to please God and walk more humbly before Him and others and are quick to see your sin and confess it.

The act of forgiveness is the necessary first step in reconciliation. It is how you are saved to reconcile your relationship with the Father through the Son as His child. Many people think forgiveness can only happen if the person accepts it. This is not necessarily true because forgiveness is an intentional decision by one person, while reconciliation involves two people and God or you and God.

The act of forgiveness is a powerful witness of your faith in your walk with God. Forgiveness is a powerful witness because it can only happen with God's help. Only God can help someone forgive because our forgiveness is modeled after God's forgiveness of our sins. Remember, Colossians 3:13 tells us to forgive as we have been forgiven.

Is there anyone that you refuse to talk to? Is there anyone you refuse to forgive? Are you disobeying God's command to forgive? Do you forgive yourself? If so, you need to be reminded of Christ's sacrifice for you and God's forgiveness of your sin against Him. Pray and ask God to help you forgive. He is always waiting for you.

Now, let's explore our final thoughts on the message: "You, Lord, are forgiving and good, abounding in love to all who call to you" (Psalm 86:5, NIV). "And when you stand praying, if you hold anything against anyone, forgive them, so that your Father in heaven may forgive you your sins" (Mark 11:25, NIV). "Blessed is the one whose transgressions are forgiven, whose sins are covered" (Psalm 32:1, NIV).

One of the most important commitments you can make as a Christian is to read your Bible every day. In each message, we will provide you with a few scriptures to look up and read on your own to plant seeds inside of you for a deeper understanding so you can grow closer to Jesus Christ through His written word.

It's time to get your Bible. For your growing with God, scriptures for the message "Who Is Blessed by Forgiveness?" are Ephesians 4:32, Mark 11:25, and 1 John 1:9.

I pray that this message create a path for you to grow closer to Jesus Christ or meet Him for the first time. It is time for you to walk away from the world and who you were that can only end in death. If you want the guaranteed passage that Jesus Christ sacrificed His life for so you could be saved as a child of God, then become who you are created to be and turn the words you read in this book into action now so you can have eternal life in the kingdom of heaven that is just waiting for you.

Planting Notes:

_____

_____

_____

_____

_____

The Three Parts of True Love

Did you know there are actually three parts of giving and receiving true love? It is so easy to get confused when they don't all work together in harmony. Each one can tell you different things at the same time, creating confusion, unless there is a way that the three parts will always work together so that you know every time what true love is.

It is amazing how most will tell you they love with their heart, but that is not true love. The heart is only one part of true love. Do you know what true love is? Have you ever given or received true love from anyone? True love is when your mind and your body love as much as your heart does. At that point, you will be able to experience and, more importantly, share what real, true love is.

The greatest form of true love that ever existed is Jesus Christ. "Why?" you might ask. God loved us more than anything in His heart, and He sent His only Son, Jesus Christ, in His image as flesh to fulfill the other two parts of love. Jesus spread the word that filled the minds of believers that they could be saved from all of their sins and be born new again into the kingdom of heaven with the Father and eternal life.

Then Jesus Christ proved His word by sacrificing His life by being beaten, tortured, and crucified on the cross to save all of us from sin and eternal damnation with His body because He loves us so much. God has given the perfect example of what the three parts of true love are.

"Love is patient, love is kind. It does not envy, it does not boast, it is not proud. It does not dishonor others, it is not self-seeking, it is not easily angered, and it keeps no record of wrongs" (1 Corinthians 13:4–5, NIV). "Above all else, guard your heart, for everything you do flows from it" (Proverbs 4:23, NIV).

You are to love the Lord with all your heart and love your neighbor as yourself. Jesus doesn't say, "These are great ideas; just get back with Me." He says that you *must* love the Lord your God with all your heart, as it is essential to living eternal life as His child.

Let me share a secret with you. Love is the breath of life that allows you to really experience the full and abundant life God has waiting for you. After all, in His presence, you are overflowing with joy and blessings forever. If you're not, then you need to get closer to God.

In the book of Psalms, we discover that in order to have overly abundant joy in our hearts, we must have the ability to overlook any challenges we face in the spirit of Christ. In order to receive the full joy a child of God can receive, we need to love Jesus Christ as He requires of us: with our mind, heart, and soul together as one.

You must understand that nothing that is easy has any value but that the discipline of obedience by your heart following God's Word brings you more than you can imagine and eternal life in the kingdom of heaven.

We have explored the heart as one part of love, so now let's explore what Scripture says about loving with the mind in Mark 12:30 (RSV), when the Lord Jesus said, "And you shall love the Lord your God with all your heart and with all your soul and with all your mind and with all your strength."

The Corinthian church idolized worldly knowledge, which did not align with the beliefs Jesus had about humanity. They were informed to conduct their faith as Jesus would because He was the pristine example of living by God's Word in the flesh in all ways, even when correction was necessary in order to follow the word of the Father.

Jesus, in His humanity, was the ideal example of someone who loved God's Word and meditated upon it. He even applied God's Word when correction needed to be given in any situation.

This is the definition of living by the Word of God in your mind, as it is applied to every area of your life as a Christian. Jesus focused on the Word; with everything He did, He first thought of doing it through the Father. So, every decision He made, regardless of the consequence, was to ensure He would always be on the right path as the Father desired.

Although it seems like something simple to do, it will be a daily challenge for us to have the mind of Christ in our lives. Jesus's use of His mind is an example to us we should follow. The resources that Jesus relied on to complete His ministry serving God are the same resources available to us in the Word of God.

Now we are going to explore loving someone with the body Christ gave you that you are to honor in His name in all that you do. The body of Christ (the church) shows the love of Christ through Christians, and it can come in many different forms. First of all, not only are you supposed to speak the words "I love You" to God but also to your brothers and sisters and all who are in your life. There will never be a day that God doesn't love you even if you walk away from Him. That is how important love is to God.

Fellowship is an instruction from God, and that is, as Christians, we need to be around one another. We need to greet and receive one another physically through Christ as He has always done for every one of us—with open arms. It is a part of love that must exist to know the real love of God and what He expects from you as His child.

You need to understand that persecution is part of loving with the body. Jesus showed the perfect example of love in His crucifixion with His body, just as you should do by allowing your former body, sins, and past to die on the cross. Not only must you love one another, but you must show it with your heart, mind, and body, just as Jesus does for you every day and will for eternity.

Let us explore our last scriptures of this message with the Word of God: "I praise you, for I am fearfully and wonderfully made" (Psalm 139:14). "For we are God's masterpiece" (Ephesians 2:10, NLT). "Therefore honor God with your bodies" (1 Corinthians 6:20, NIV). We now know that to understand, feel, and give the love of God, it must be with your heart, mind, and body—the three parts of love.

One of the most important commitments you can make as a Christian is to read your Bible every day. In each message, we will provide you with a few scriptures to look up and read on your own to plant seeds inside of you for a deeper understanding so you can grow closer to Jesus Christ through His written word.

It's time to get your Bible. For your growing with God, scriptures for the message "The Three Parts of True Love" are Matthew 4:1, John 17:11, and Luke 4:14–18.

I pray that this message creates a path for you to grow closer to Jesus Christ or meet Him for the first time. If you want to receive the guaranteed passage that He sacrificed Himself on the cross for so you can be saved as a child of God, then become who you are created to be and turn the words you read in this book into action now so you can have eternal life in the kingdom of heaven that is just waiting for you.

Planting Notes:

_____

_____

_____

_____

_____

It's Not What You Know; It's Who You Know

You can be the most intelligent person in the world, but it may seem that some people receive special treatment just because of someone they know and not what they know: like with the invitation to the country club, the good ole boy network, high society clubs, etc., which only creates division among all of those who are equals.

"It's not what you know; it's who you know"—I have heard many people say this. Have you ever heard that saying before? About a job? Getting into an organization? Getting a promotion? It is as if you can know everything there is to know, and it doesn't matter unless you know the right person to help you accomplish what you are trying to do. Do you feel this is true? Do people really show favor to one over others?

Do you think if you know every word of the Bible, you are saved? Do you think if you do good works, you are saved? Do you think if you go to church, you are saved? Do you think you are born again because of what you know or who you know?

It is really simple, as it does not matter what you know; it matters who you know, and if you don't know Jesus Christ and have a relationship with Him, then you will never be saved.

Do you know Jesus says to come to Him and to know Him? Not to just know about Him but to *know Him* and have a relationship with Him. This is the only way you are saved: through knowing the Son, as it is not good enough that you just know about Him; you must know Him by having a relationship with Him.

Now we are going to explore some scriptures that show us that you must know God and have a relationship with Him and not just know of Him or about Him, starting with 1 John 4:6: "We are from God. Whoever knows God listens to us; whoever is not from God does not listen to us. By this we know the Spirit of truth and the spirit of error."

What a great verse that reassures us that we are from God and that we must know God so He will hear us when we speak to Him or through Him to others. By having a relationship with God, you will be able to know what is holy and what is ungodly in your walk as His child—another clear path on the road to the kingdom of heaven.

We will now explore the scripture of John 17:3: "And this is eternal life, that they know you, the only true God, and Jesus Christ whom you have sent."

What an amazing gift from God of eternal life and all the blessings that come with it! It is more than you can ever imagine, but once again: it is clearly written there is only one way to experience everything God has waiting for you as His child, and that is to know Him through the Son whom He sent for your salvation on His behalf so you may know Him and love Him and not just know about Him.

Knowing someone is what makes them real in your life and not just a passing thought. You can know something about this person and something about that person, but until you have a relationship with one of them, you never know them or who they are or why they are in your life. But God makes it very clear why He is in your life.

Knowing someone makes them part of you, as we all take parts of everyone we ever meet in our lives with us. The problem is you can take good parts or bad parts of people inside of you. But the good news is you get to make a choice about what parts you want to become you as a whole person. The only way to do that correctly is by Jesus Christ living inside of you and you knowing Him.

We will continue our scriptures with John 14:6: "Jesus said to him, 'I am the way, and the truth, and the life. No one comes to the Father except through me.'"

There is no misunderstanding of this verse: it is clear directions on how to reach God through Jesus, with first the direction "I am the way" so you will never be lost again. The second one is that you always know God only speaks the truth, "I am the truth," and anything He says to you or has you do is for your best so you can become who He intends you to be. And the third one is eternal life, "I am the life," in the kingdom of heaven, and one will not enter it if they do not know Jesus Christ.

Let's make this crystal clear: God is not saying, "If you have heard of Jesus," "If you have read about Him," or "If you read your Bible." None of that matters until you confess your sins, ask for forgiveness to be saved, and have that very personal relationship with Jesus Christ where you know Him as He does you now because He lives inside of you as the light of you as a child of God, burning bright for all to see.

In our closing scripture, we are exploring John 3:16: "For God so loved the world, that he gave his only Son, that whoever believes in him should not perish but have eternal life."

If you are a Christian, you know this scripture says it all. God loved us so much and wanted us to know Him so badly that He sent His only Son to be sacrificed on the cross, and anyone, and that means leaving no one out, who believes in Him will not die but have eternal life in heaven. Praise the Lord! God is so good to show us a defined, proven path to be all He has intended us to be as His children.

Remember: you can only experience love, trust, wisdom, guidance, forgiveness, grace, mercy, and everything else that is a blessing when you have a relationship with anyone and know who they are and they know you. That is all God the Father wants—to have a relationship with you as His child and the miracle He brought into His creation.

One of the most important commitments you can make as a Christian is to read your Bible every day. In each message, we will provide you with a few scriptures to look up and read on your own

to plant seeds inside of you for a deeper understanding so you can grow closer to Jesus Christ through His written word.

It's time to get your Bible. For your growing with God, scriptures for the message "It's Not What You Know; It's Who You Know" are John 2:5–6, Proverbs 9:10, and Matthew 11:27–28.

I pray that this message creates a path for you to grow closer to Jesus Christ or meet Him for the first time. If you want to receive the guaranteed passage that He sacrificed Himself on the cross for so you can be saved as a child of God, then become who you are created to be and turn the words you read in this book into action now so you can have eternal life in the kingdom of heaven that is just waiting for you.

Planting Notes:

_____

_____

_____

_____

_____

Are You Stuck in the Comfort Zone?

Do you ever feel like your life is in a rut, going nowhere, with no plans for your future? Do you do the same things every day and expect different results? Does your spiritual life seem like it has no spirit? Is there any purpose for your life?

Are you stuck in your comfort zone? Are you comfortably numb? Has your life become stale? Are you doing the same thing all the time? Has your growth as a Christian come to a stop? Do you ever wonder that there has to be more that God has intended for you? Are you following the same footsteps that Jesus did? If not, there is your starting place.

The truth is you can be saved, attend church, fellowship, work, and do the things that have become normal in your life, but you may not be growing as God intends you to. Doesn't He command us to become "fishers of men" (meaning reaching out to everyone you do not know)? Do you think Jesus had one normal day in His life when He was sent by God to complete what was necessary to save you, where He just did the same thing every day with the same people?

Jesus's life was never the same thing every day. He was never stuck in a comfort zone. Can you imagine the amount of growth Jesus had as a child of God on His way to the cross? Yes, Jesus was with His disciples every day, but He met them one by one and brought them to Him to meet the Father, just as you are supposed to do with others.

So, we all must understand that if we keep doing the same things and expecting different results, that will never happen. You do not grow by doing the same thing. If you had not stepped out in faith, you would have never been saved and growing as a Christian. So you came out of your comfort zone and walked into the arms of Jesus Christ, and that is exactly what you are supposed to lead others to do as well. That is how you grow as a child of God: through others you have never met.

How ashamed would you feel to meet God at heaven's gate and not have one soul that you have brought with you after everything He has done for you? Of course, we want to keep all of our spiritual connections in everything we do, but we must expand those to others.

How else do you grow a kingdom if others are not coming with you? Jesus literally met and saved new believers daily, and yet all who know Him are with Him always and forever. This is what you should do as a child of God and what you were made for.

Let's look at the scripture of Isaiah 58:10: "If you pour yourself out for the hungry and satisfy the desire of the afflicted, then shall your light rise in the darkness and your gloom be as the noonday." This scripture tells you exactly how to get out of your comfort zone: by putting all of who you are into the betterment of others, finding the lost, the lonely, the hurt, the unwanted, and the unsaved, and showing them the way as you were shown to meet Jesus Christ. By doing so, you are definitely pleasing God and growing as a Christian and growing what He has in store for your eternal life here and with Him in heaven.

Next, we will visit the scripture of Matthew 5:16: "In the same way, let your light shine before others, that they may see your good deeds and glorify your Father in heaven."

This scripture is teaching you how to attract others to you as Jesus attracted you. Have you ever heard someone say, "There's just something different about that person; I can't figure out what it is, but something is interesting"? It is usually a Christian they are talking about.

Most of the time, the one speaking is usually a person who may be lost, and they see the light of God inside of you and feel it when they are around you. They are looking for directions (even if they do not know it), and you are a beacon for them to find their way home, just as what Jesus did for you.

Our scripture concluding this message will be Proverbs 3:27 (NIV): "Do not withhold good from those to whom it is due, when it is in your power to act."

This scripture has a wide meaning of how it applies to us as Christians. If we see someone doing God's work, then we should encourage them in what they are doing. But more importantly, if you meet someone that is lost, you are to show them the way to Jesus, as it is their right to have the choice of eternal life and your responsibility to show them the way.

Because you have been saved and are walking with God daily as you are growing as His child, He has given you the same power as Jesus to show others who He is, and it is your responsibility to fulfill what you have been created for in His image and likeness in all ways.

What does all of what we have been speaking about in this message mean? You are never to be in a comfort zone as a Christian or become comfortably numb in your walk with God. You are designed in His image and to do exactly as He does. Jesus gave us the example of what to follow to perfection so that all we would have to do is listen, read, learn, follow, share, and grow in the Word of God on the path to the kingdom of heaven and bring as many brothers and sisters as we can with us.

One of the most important commitments you can make as a Christian is to read your Bible every day. In each message, we will provide you with a few scriptures to look up and read on your own to plant seeds inside of you for a deeper understanding so you can grow closer to Jesus Christ through His written word.

It's time to get your Bible. For your growing with God, scriptures for the message "Are You Stuck in the Comfort Zone?" are Romans 10:1, Luke 14:23, and Matthew 5:14–16.

I pray that this message creates a path for you to grow closer to Jesus Christ or meet Him for the first time. If you want to receive the guaranteed passage that He sacrificed Himself on the cross for so you can be saved as a child of God, then become who you are created to be and turn the words you read in this book into action now so you can have eternal life in the kingdom of heaven that is just waiting for you.

Planting Notes:

_____

_____

_____

_____

_____

Do You Take Your Problems to God, or Do You Take God to Your Problems?

People who have problems in their life actually have two different ways they can handle them. Most seem to do the same thing and just complain about their circumstances. They may even pray about their problems. So, that provokes a question: Is there a correct way to pray about your problems to God for Him to hear you?

What do you do when you have a problem in your life? Do you complain about it? Do you get upset? Do you get discouraged? Do you lose your faith? Do you pray to God (humble and explaining your circumstances and asking for His will to be done) or at God (venting and demanding He fix your problems)? How do you deal with your problems as a child of God? Do you tell God about all of your problems, worries, stress and ask Him to fix everything?

Do you know the right way to deal with your problems as a child of God? Do you know that you are not supposed to complain, get upset, get discouraged, lose your faith, pray *at* God, fret over your worries, your stress, etc., that comes from your problems?

As you are a Christian, all of that negative emotion that Satan uses to chip away at your faith and soul is not yours to own; it belongs to God the second you become saved. You are to lay it down and stay in the joy and love God has placed you in through the sacrifice of the Son.

You are absolutely to lay every problem in your life in the hands of God immediately, without reservation, and let the Father deal with the problems to help His child grow as it should. You are not to allow the emotions of the world to taint your spirit and soil your soul, trying to pull you away from God and your destiny in heaven.

How do you take your problems to God? Do you tell Him what your problems are, complain about them, and ask Him to fix them? Or do you pray to God and say, "Lord, I know You are there for my protection and You will take care of the circumstances in my life in Your time. Please, Lord, please give me the strength and faith to remain in Your joy and grace as You direct my life where only You know I should be. I will not fret or worry but stay in faith and love knowing that You are always there for me with only the best for my life as Your child"?

Now let's look at God's Word about how you, as a Christian, are instructed to deal with your problems:

> Do not be anxious about anything, but in everything by prayer and supplication with thanksgiving let your requests be made known to God. And the peace of God, which surpasses all understanding, will guard your hearts and your minds in Christ Jesus.
>
> Philippians 4:6–7

This scripture is a love song about what God is willing to do to protect you because He loves you so much. He removes the attacks on you by His Holy Spirit with your prayer and thankfulness. You know the Savior is your soldier that battles every enemy that comes against you in life. You know that you will forever be covered in faith and peace because of who you are in Christ for eternity.

Now we will explore the scripture of Proverbs 3:5–6: "Trust in the LORD with all your heart, and do not lean on your own understanding. In all your ways acknowledge him, and he will make straight your paths."

First, we need to understand that trusting God, especially with your heart, means that you have a relationship with Him, as trust is earned in a relationship. Your faith is so strong in Him that you have walked away from the ways of the world. You only lean on Him to provide direction and know He is there with you always. If you lay your problems down to Him, walk away from them in every way, and let God deal with them, then He will keep you from being lost and on His path of life as His child.

In our closing scripture in this message, we will explore Isaiah 41:10: "Fear not, for I am with you; be not dismayed, for I am your God; I will strengthen you, I will help you, I will uphold you with my righteous right hand."

This scripture is so clear and simple for you to follow His Word. You are not to fear anything, and He is always by your side. Worry has never solved one problem and is no longer a part of who you are because there is no problem too big for God to handle. He is always there with strength for you; He will always help you, no matter where you are, and protect you with His right hand of righteousness. What is at God's right hand that is righteous? Jesus Christ, who He has sent for you.

Now let's look at some simple steps to laying down your problems to God and not yourself. How do you actually give God your problems?

Your first step is to recognize you're always blessed and not cursed and have a way that guarantees to take care of anything for you if you bring it to God and lay it down for Him to deal with.

What should you do next? Always look up for guidance from God!

The third step is to not rate your worries by the level of importance you feel they are: sometimes, one problem seems bigger than another, so you give that one the most attention when all of them are not yours to deal with if you are a child of God.

The fourth step is you must learn to discard your concern over any problems and know that God is at work all the time. The fifth step is to pray, pray, and pray some more to remove your concerns so that you stay where God needs you to be so that He hears you. Finally, you must allow God to soften your heart to remain in the peace He has for you in your eternal life with Him here and in the kingdom of heaven.

A final thought is to make sure you always keep God as your first priority in everything you think, say, or do, as anything else is not what a child of God would do to honor what He has sacrificed you.

One of the most important commitments you can make as a Christian is to read your Bible every day. In each message, we will provide you with a few scriptures to look up and read on your own to plant seeds inside of you for a deeper understanding so you can grow closer to Jesus Christ through His written word.

It's time to get your Bible. For your growing with God, scriptures for the message "Do You Take Your Problems to God, or Do You Take God to Your Problems?" are Nahum 1:7, Matthew 11:28–30, and John 14:27.

I pray that this message creates a path for you to grow closer to Jesus Christ or meet Him for the first time. If you want to receive the guaranteed passage that He sacrificed Himself on the cross for so you can be saved as a child of God, then become who you are created to be and turn the words you read in this book into action now so you can have eternal life in the kingdom of heaven that is just waiting for you.

Planting Notes:

_____

_____

_____

_____

_____

What Is Perfect Obedience?

Because we are all children of God, we are expected to be obedient in all ways according to His Word. But for so many, the line to where obedience and disobedience meet seems to be blurred, making people feel like they are being obedient when they are not. Often, correction enters their life due to their inconscient disobedience, and they don't even understand why. There is no gray area when it comes to being obedient as a child of God.

Let's get started! So, what is perfect obedience? First, we need to understand that perfect obedience does not question, ever. If you question the instruction of authority in your life that is holy, godly and is there to protect and guide you, then you are being completely disobedient and committing a sin.

How do you know if you are being obedient or not? Good news! It's already written out for you in the Bible how to be obedient on your path to eternal life once you are saved. If you or others around you act in any way other than what the Word of God says, you should not be doing whatever it is you're doing or be involved with anyone in any way, acting in such a manner. You are willfully participating in disobedience.

It is disobedience, and you are to separate yourself from it as a child of God. This is a perfect example of how important it is for you to read and know your Bible. After all, it is the instructions for your eternal life unless you are interested in the other option of living under correction and ultimately dying in this world.

All of us know what being disobedient is. Every one of us got in trouble with our parents because we did something we were told not to do. Children have forever been told by a teacher to stop doing what they are doing if they misbehave. Some of us disrespect others, our spouses and parents. All are examples of what perfect disobedience is. You must learn what to do in your walk with God, but you must also learn what not to do in your footsteps as you grow in Christ.

As you leave behind you a path of the steps you take glorifying Christ, you should take each with great care to ensure you are acting as Jesus would. We are always a witness to the results of the love of God in our lives. We only experience results by something that has happened to us, which God directed without notice to us. We don't always see the will of God by looking ahead of us, as God only knows what the future holds.

We see the love of God in our lives by looking back over our shoulder at what He has done for us, even if it was just one minute ago. We all should stay in obedience without the knowledge of what the Father has in store for now and the future. No one knows what opportunities God has planned for us.

All of us are human and born of sin, with absolutely no obedience, except what the world outlines for us if we are not saved. As we continue to grow with God and stumble occasionally, we must understand that the ways of God are often unexplained. The way of God is usually not even seen.

Our faith is our guide through the Word of God. Because faith is obedience defined and knowing that God always has your best interest, no matter what season He has you in life, it is true obedience as His child in all ways that shows Him your love for Him.

Why are obedience and disobedience so important to understand? Because you will have a life full of blessing or correction, and you need to understand what you did and why it is happening. After all, you are what your actions are. Look at what Jesus Christ did for you!

Let's look at what the Bible says about obedience and disobedience.

We will start with Luke 6:46: "Why do you call me 'Lord, Lord,' and not do what I tell you?" God is very displeased with your disobedience in this scripture, as you called for Him but did not follow as He instructed you to do in His Word.

He is concerned as to why you are calling on Him if you are not going to follow His Word. If a child of God acts in this manner, I would fully expect God to lead you in the direction of correction as a reminder of His love for you and to clear up your understanding of what obedience is and that you are to abide by His Word.

We will continue with the scripture of Romans 5:19: "For as by the one man's disobedience the many were made sinners, so by the one man's obedience the many will be made righteous." This scripture shows the power that one person's actions of disobedience lead other people to death in the world or eternal life in heaven.

We will conclude our scriptures in this message with Joshua 1:8:

> This Book of the Law shall not depart from your mouth,
> but you shall meditate on it day and night, so that you
> may be careful to do according to all that is written in it.
> For then you will make your way prosperous, and then
> you will have good success.

What a powerful scripture about reading and knowing the Bible in your heart, mind, and soul! Your every word and breath is the air of the Lord shining inside of you, healing you, loving you, and always with you. God is who you are, and in all you do, and has clearly given you simple-to-follow instructions so He may bless you as His child.

As a final thought: always remember that the word of God in the Bible and faith are your guiding light with Jesus Christ. As a child of God, you are to stay in obedience always. You must understand that there is no need to question God and fall into disobedience, as anything He does is done to perfection whether you or I understand it or not, as He is our true Father.

We are to obey Him always and, in return, show the love He has already given us that we do not deserve. Always remember that love is perfect obedience and perfect obedience is love.

One of the most important commitments you can make as a Christian is to read your Bible every day. In each message, we will provide you with scriptures to look up and read for a deeper understanding, planting seeds inside of you for you to grow closer to Jesus Christ.

It's time to get your Bible. For your growing with God, scriptures for the message "What is Perfect Obedience?" are 1 Peter 1:14, Romans 13:1, and Hebrews 13:17.

I pray that this message creates a path for you to grow closer to Jesus Christ or meet Him for the first time. If you want to receive the guaranteed passage that He sacrificed Himself on the cross for so you can be saved as a child of God, then become who you are created to be and turn the words you read in this book into action now so you can have eternal life in the kingdom of heaven that is just waiting for you.

Planting Notes:

_____

_____

_____

_____

_____

The Circle of Life

Often people miss out on blessings because they have not completed the circle of life by doing what God ultimately created them for. Most will think the circle of life has to do with birth and death, but in reality, it does not. It has to do with being saved through Christ and what is expected of you.

We are going to explore the circle of life for us as Christians and children of God. We will begin with our understanding that we know our relationship with God should be the most important one in our life. There are many other relationships we have that we want to model exactly after our relationship with the Lord and Savior because Jesus will offer salvation to anyone who comes to Him by themselves or through you.

It is just a fact that some will never have a relationship with God, no matter how much they see your life being blessed or how unfortunate things that they cannot explain will always be occurring in their life. You, as a child of God, will always and forever try to bring others to Jesus, no matter what circle of life they are in with you.

We have four circles of life relationships, and they are our innermost circle, our inner circle, our outer circle, and our outermost circle of life relationships. Someone may start in your outermost circle and end up in your innermost circle with you and God.

The great thing is that we can change and go from the outermost circle to the innermost circle, which allows us to have a relationship with the Father, and once you are saved, your relationship stays the same forever in the innermost circle of your life with Him.

The circle of life is like a relationship target, and in the center that takes perfect aim to contact is God. When you are aiming and connecting with your target right in the center, you are right there in the innermost part of your circle of life that is just for your relationship with God and exactly where He wants you to be as His child.

So, we have a clear understanding the first circle of life relationship you have is the innermost circle and that space is reserved just for you and God alone so that He has that one-on-one loving relationship with you that He desires.

Let's explore the scripture of John 1:10–13:

> He was in the world, and the world was made through him, yet the world did not know him. He came to his own, and his own people did not receive him. But to all who did receive him, who believed in his name, he gave the right to become children of God, who were born, not of blood nor of the will of the flesh nor of the will of man, but of God.

As we look into our next circle of life, we are talking about our spouses, children, and family that make up this circle of life that is right next to God and you, which is your inner circle of life. This circle contains the most important people who are directly in your life, to who you give the greatest amount of your life so that they know you love them.

These are people you spend most of your life with, create most of your memories with, share the most challenges and blessings with, and automatically share love with. This inner circle of life is usually the people who are closest to you, next to your relationship with God. They are people you love in the same way that God loves you.

Now let's visit our next scripture of Matthew 19:4–6:

> Have you not read that he who created them from the beginning made them male and female, and said, "Therefore a man shall leave his father and his mother and hold fast to his wife, and the two shall become one flesh"? So

they are no longer two but one flesh. What therefore God has joined together, let not man separate.

Next, we will explore your outer circle of life. These people are other believers, your friends, and your coworkers, people you occasionally spend time with and have a familiar relationship with. These people you fellowship and worship with as well as your inner circle. These are people who affect your life the most and are not in your inner circle of life.

As we continue with our scriptures, let's explore Ecclesiastes 4:9–12:

> Two are better than one, because they have a good reward for their toil. For if they fall, one will lift up his fellow. But woe to him who is alone when he falls and has not another to lift him up! Again, if two lie together, they keep warm, but how can one keep warm alone? And though a man might prevail against one who is alone, two will withstand him—a threefold cord is not quickly broken.

The final circle of life we will explore is your outermost circle that includes the rest of the world, people you do not know and have not met yet, acquaintances, people who pass by you, and who you pass by in life. You have no relationship with these people as they are strangers. Some may be believers, and some may not, but they are usually the people you are to reach out to and bring home with you to meet Jesus.

Let's visit our final scripture in this message, 1 John 2:15–17:

> Do not love the world or the things in the world. If anyone loves the world, the love of the Father is not in him. For all that is in the world—the desires of the flesh and the desires of the eyes and pride in possessions—is not from the Father but is from the world. And the world is passing away along with its desires, but whoever does the will of God abides forever.

It is important to understand the circles of life so you can know the order in which your relationships should be in your life and who always comes first. You also need to know what relationships you need to focus on to bring them closer to God and do what He has created you for.

The *key* is how many times you can contact the center of the target and bring others to meet Jesus from the outermost circle in your innermost circle. No matter where your aim goes in your circle of relationships in bringing others to the Lord and Savior, you always know one thing. You are on target, and eventually, your aim will be perfect for bringing others to meet Jesus. The key is to never stop trying, never give up, never quit, and do as Jesus did, giving your all for the salvation of others in every circle of life.

Understanding your relationships in the circle of life is important to grow as a Christian in order for you to know where you are in your walk with God and where others that may need a little help along the way are. One thing you know about the circle of life is: no matter where anyone falls in it, we are all together with God at the center of the circle of life of anyone who believes and receives the Father, the Son, and the Holy Spirit.

It is important to realize the circle of life has a beginning; God dreamed it, imagined it, planned it, designed it, engineered it, and created it, and then, when God's hand took the dust of the earth and created humans, He breathed into existence the beginning of the circle of life.

As a final thought: regardless of what circle of life people fall into, you are supposed to love all of them as God loves you. The circle of life is the process that takes place to bring someone out of the world full of death in sin, which is in the outermost circle of life, into the innermost circle of life in Christ—out of the darkness and into the light. Christ is always to be the center of the lives of all of us.

So, in review, we understand we have four different circles of life relationships that are: your innermost circle in your relationship with God; your inner circle is your relationships with your spouse, children, and entire family; your outer circle relationships are with other believers, friends, coworkers, or those you are casually familiar with; and your outermost circle is people of the world, those you do not know and just pass by, but who are usually the ones that need to know Jesus the most.

Make sure you are ready in your circle of life relationship with God, as we have learned that everything that has a beginning in the circle of life also has an ending, and He is on His way back very soon.

One of the most important commitments you can make as a Christian is to read your Bible every day. In each message, we will provide you with a few scriptures to look up and read on your own to plant seeds inside of you for a deeper understanding so you can grow closer to Jesus Christ through His written word.

It's time to get your Bible. For your growing with God, scriptures for the message "The Circle of Life" are 1 Corinthians 15:33, 2 Corinthians 6:14, and 1 Corinthians 5:1.

I pray that this message creates a path for you to grow closer to Jesus Christ or meet Him for the first time. If you want to receive the guaranteed passage that He sacrificed Himself on the cross for so you can be saved as a child of God, then become who you are created to be and turn the words you read in this book into action now so you can have eternal life in the kingdom of heaven that is just waiting for you.

Planting Notes:

_____

_____

_____

_____

_____

Are You Walking on a Fence?

Isn't it incredible when you can perform amazing feats of balance where you can live your life on a tight rope and think you're not going to fall off? There are many people who are doing just enough, and the bare minimum or walking in the gray area of life gives them a pass on how they can live.

In this message, we are going to take a deep dive into the inner you. So, let's begin with a few questions to ask yourself. In order to take in the knowledge that God will share with you, you must open your heart with honesty to receive His will for you.

What type of fence are you walking on? Do you walk a fine line in everything you do? Do you live your life in gray areas in who you are? Are you in a bar Saturday night and church Sunday morning? Are you late or not following through with everything you commit yourself to? What is your word to others worth to you? Does your Bible only open in church? Do you talk about God away from church? Do you even go to church?

Do you know God commits to you in the same way you do to Him?

Do you want God walking on the fence about you as His child? Or do you want God committed to your well-being always? So, let me ask you: Do you know you must be there for God for Him to be there for you?

So, what does "be there" for God mean? Have you asked Jesus Christ to forgive you and repented from your sins so you can be saved? Do you want to be a child of God with eternal life in the kingdom of heaven? If you want God to be there for you, then this action comes first; otherwise, you are just walking the fence and will fall off of it sooner or later.

If you haven't asked to be saved by Christ, then please listen: I care about you enough that I have to ask you why you are walking the fence on your own salvation? Why are you waiting to be saved? Do you think you have forever to be born again? Do you not love yourself? Do you feel unworthy?

Are you trapped in the ways of the world? Do you worship idols and don't even know it? Do you know if your heart is disciplined for God, you suffer pain for those that are lost? Just as Jesus did for you on the cross.

Do you even know when you are walking the fence, you are flirting with death and eternal life? Do you know the more you walk the fence, the further it takes you away from God?

Do you think you can play in the dark and still walk in the light? What is your salvation worth to you? Do your purpose and destiny matter to you? What will happen to you if you keep walking the fence in your life?

Let's find out and explore the fence that can cause you to fall daily in your walk with God, and that is temptation. One very important thing you must learn—listen—you don't want to miss this: you must understand temptation only succeeds when your heart is unprepared for it. How is your heart prepared for temptation?

There is only one way to do that. You are saved and following the Word of God in obedience as His child. Let's look at Scripture about where your desires are supposed to be fulfilled instead of you walking the fence on your salvation. Psalm 37:4 says, "Delight yourself in the LORD, and he will give you the desires of your heart."

God has made it really simple to get all your heart desires. Find the joy in your life in your relationship with the Lord, and the desires of your heart will be given to you according to His Word. Remember: blessings are a two-way street.

God feels blessed by your love and commitment to Christ, and your total obedience pleases Him so much that He wants to give you all that your heart desires and things you cannot even imagine here and in heaven where He is waiting for you to come home.

The only way to have true joy is if all of your desires manifest themselves through Jesus Christ inside of you and if you allow Him to bless you instead of you taking control and allowing false images offered by the world that are only there for your damnation.

As we continue, let's look at another fence that you walk that can cause you to fall every single day. That is discipline, which is one of the most challenging parts of being a child of a God. But ultimately, it is the Word of God that defines who you are and what is expected of you from the Father.

We are made to be disciples, which is the action of discipline to the Word of God in life. It is your sole purpose to share the Word of God with others to bring them to Jesus Christ. If you choose not to do that and it is not done in your walk in life, then you are not becoming the person God has intended for you to be as His child.

Now let's explore Scripture on discipline with Deuteronomy 8:5–6:

> Know then in your heart that, as a man disciplines his son, the LORD your God disciplines you. So you shall keep the commandments of the LORD your God by walking in his ways and by fearing him.

In this verse, you learn, by God living inside of you, His child, that He expects you to not only follow His Word but lead others in the same way He has you. You are His child and are subject to any necessary correction for not keeping His commandments. This will continue through the discipline of His love for you until you have learned and become what is expected of you.

As a final thought: we have just touched on a couple of fences that you can walk in your life. The key is to recognize those fences before you ever step your foot on one and take the chance of falling and having your life devastated by Satan, all because you gave him an opportunity by wavering in your faith in God and not trusting Him completely. The only way you can guarantee you will see all the fences that come in your life is to read your Bible and know the Word of God. That way, you just go around them and stay on the ground, walking with God and not putting your life at risk as His child, which, otherwise, would cause Him to correct the situation because He loves you so much.

One of the most important commitments you can make as a Christian is to read your Bible every day. In each message, we will provide you with a few scriptures to look up and read on your own to plant seeds inside of you for a deeper understanding so you can grow closer to Jesus Christ through His written word.

It's time to get your Bible. For your growing with God, scriptures for the message "Are You Walking on a Fence?" are Hebrews 12:11, 1 Corinthians 10:13, and Ephesians 6:10–1.

I pray that this message creates a path for you to grow closer to Jesus Christ or meet Him for the first time. If you want to receive the guaranteed passage that He sacrificed Himself on the cross for so you can be saved as a child of God, then become who you are created to be and turn the words you read in this book into action now so you can have eternal life in the kingdom of heaven that is just waiting for you.

Planting Notes:

_____

_____

_____

_____

_____

Do You Change the World, or Does the World Change You?

The world seems to have changed at the speed of light since time began. We have gone from wagons and horseback in just over the last hundred years alone to taking space vacations—in just that short span of time. How do you determine what is being done in the name of humanity or in the name of Jesus Christ and what you should know and do?

Let's begin and ask ourselves these questions: Do you change the world? Or does the world change you? We are all made in the image of God as Jesus was. Do you do the same things Jesus does? Do you do things that would change the world in the way God has commanded it to be done?

Do you follow God's commandments? Do you know that Christians lead by example as Jesus did? Do you follow the ways of the world in becoming who you are? Do you share worldly views with others? Do you share the Word of God and its views with others? What do you do currently to change the world? Do your actions honor God, or do they idolize the world?

So, what we need to discover is if you are a child of God or a child of the world. Do you know the life of Jesus was created and sacrificed for one reason only: to change the world and all who live in it? If we are made in His image, then that is what every one of us is supposed to do to honor what has been done for us.

But how do you change the world? The same way Jesus did: by your actions, with what you speak and do. Your actions are your full commitment of yourself to a purpose. It is one thing to have a thought but entirely another to act on it and follow through with your commitment. This is the only way you can change anything for good or bad.

The most important way to change the world is you must change yourself first. If you are not saved and a child of God, it is time that you walk away from the darkness and come into the light of eternal life—right now. Otherwise, you are a child of the world, spreading the message that will only lead you and anyone that is influenced by your actions to death.

Let's look at some ways you can change the world as a child of God through your actions. Remember: actions only carry value to others when they see them and are shared with others.

Do you read your Bible with others? Do you talk about Jesus to others? Do you do good works for others? Do you put the needs of others before your own? Do you invite others to church? Do you fellowship and go to Bible studies? Do you have your own fellow-shipping group? Do you ask others if they are sure they would go to heaven if they died today?

It is all in your actions that determine your destiny. Listen: if you don't commit to the action of asking Jesus for forgiveness and that you want to repent of your sins and be saved, then you will never be saved. Your action changes the world for good or bad and determines your ultimate ending.

Now let's see what the Bible says about you changing the world. We will start with the scripture of Matthew 28:18–20 (NIV):

> Then Jesus came to them and said, "All authority in heaven and on earth has been given to me. Therefore go and make disciples of all nations, baptizing them in the name of the Father and of the Son and of the Holy Spirit, and teaching them to obey everything I have commanded you. And surely I am with you always, to the very end of the age."

These are clear directions on what we are supposed to do to change the world in the way that God wants it to be. Jesus is transferring His power from God to you to do as He does, and He will be with you through eternity. He instructs you to change the lives of others as yours has been changed.

Understand that the voice of Jesus was so powerful it changed the world forever. That is, one of the most powerful actions you can do to change the world is to speak the Word of God to everyone.

Let's look at the scripture of Hebrews 4:12 (NLT):

> For the word of God is alive and powerful. It is sharper than the sharpest two-edged sword, cutting between soul and spirit, between joint and marrow. It exposes our innermost thoughts and desires.

All the time, unbelievers struggle, trying to debate the truth of Scripture. Jesus used Scripture when He was tempted by Satan in the desert. So, remember: you can do as Jesus does and use the Word of God to help you change the world, as it is the one thing that always exposes the truth about everything in your life and others.

It is a fact that God's Word applies to every area of life throughout any century, as it shows us in the scripture of Hebrews 13:8 that says, "Jesus Christ is the same yesterday and today and forever." Now listen: this is very important, so you don't want to miss this. The Word of God is the only thing that will never change, but it is also the only thing that can change everything, including you and the world.

As we continue with the scriptures, we will explore what God says in Isaiah 55:11 (NLT): "My word. I send it out, and it always produces fruit. It will accomplish all I want it to, and it will prosper everywhere I send it." You never know when you have the opportunity to plant a seed in someone's mind that God will use to change that person's life forever and the world.

The scripture we will conclude this message with is Matthew 5:16 (NIV): "In the same way, let your light shine before others, that they may see your good deeds and glorify your Father in heaven."

As a final thought: you must realize God loves you and trusts you so much that not only did He sacrifice His only Son for your salvation, but He put the fate of His kingdom in your hands to help Him change the world and turn it away from sin so His beloved children can come home with you. Don't condone or compromise. Be always reminded that Jesus didn't come to sanctify the world's ways; He came to save the world from its ways.

The most important thing you must remember is whose world you are building, the kingdom of heaven for God or hell for Satan? All of your actions will be building one or the other all the time. The *world is in darkness, so let your light shine* to create a path for others to follow, and the world will change as God intended. It's all up to you.

One of the most important commitments you can make as a Christian is to read your Bible every day. In each message, we will provide you with a few scriptures to look up and read on your own to plant seeds inside of you for a deeper understanding so you can grow closer to Jesus Christ through His written word.

It's time to get your Bible. For your growing with God, scriptures for the message "Do You Change the World, or Does the World Change You?" are Malachi 3:6, Genesis 3:17–19, and James 1:17.

I pray that this message creates a path for you to grow closer to Jesus Christ or meet Him for the first time. If you want to receive the guaranteed passage that He sacrificed Himself on the cross for so you can be saved as a child of God, then become who you are created to be and turn the words you read in this book into action now so you can have eternal life in the kingdom of heaven that is just waiting for you.

Planting Notes:

_____

_____

_____

_____

_____

BIRDS OF A FEATHER FLOCK TOGETHER

Have you ever noticed how groups of birds fly in almost an arrow type of formation, going in several directions? It is amazing, as each one stays in sync with all the others, without getting lost, because they have become one in the air, together, and have a direction in which they follow in unity.

I am sure we have all heard this saying of "birds of a feather flock together" before. But what does it mean? Is there a message we should all learn from? After all, everything is created by God for a reason and a purpose. Let's explore the meaning of the words in their singular form and see if we find God in there.

First, we'll look at the word "birds," not "bird," not singular or alone but "birds" (many, groups, multiples). So, we can see that we are talking about several, hundreds, thousands, and millions in this world, without limit, that could be in any location anywhere in the world. Kind of like Christians are.

Now let's move on to the next part of the statement, "of a feather." This is pointing out a specific type of being that is similar to or like one another, possibly created by one image. Kind of like a dove, or an angel to one another, or as we would be to Jesus. Ever wonder why a dove is a holy image? They all look alike and all gather together.

Let's look at the next part of the statement, which is "flock." We discover that the meaning of the word is (okay, listen carefully) one kind that is feeding, resting, or traveling together. We are fed the Word of God to fill us up with peaceful rest.

And our destination and purpose are to multiply who we are in Christ as one, as we all go through time as one body of Christ on the way home to eternal life in the kingdom of heaven.

We will look at the last part of this statement, the word "together," which means to create companionship or close association. This is exactly what Christians do, what is commanded by the Word of God. The relationship with God and one another is the most important part of being a Christian.

It is where everything begins: by asking Jesus to forgive you, repent of your sins, and be saved. When Jesus forgives you and you are born again, you now have a relationship with God the Father, God the Son, and God the Holy Spirit that is your guaranty of eternal life in the kingdom.

So, we have learned that "birds of a feather flock together" means that Christians in the likeness of one another are to gather, fellowship, worship, reach out to others for Christ in places we have not been, and be fed by the Word of God so that they and we experience peace and rest. We love one another through the love of God as He loves us.

Now we will explore Scripture about why God commands the gathering of His children together. We will begin with 1 John 1:3:

> That which we have seen and heard we proclaim also to you, so that you too may have fellowship with us; and indeed our fellowship is with the Father and with his Son Jesus Christ.

Everything we have learned in our walk with God, from the very beginning of asking for forgiveness and to be saved, we are to share with everyone and bring them home to Jesus Christ. Then we can come together as one in fellowship and worship with the Lord and Savior.

The next scripture we explore will be Hebrews 10:24–25:

> And let us consider how to stir up one another to love and good works, not neglecting to meet together, as is

the habit of some, but encouraging one another, and all the more as you see the Day drawing near.

This is such a blessing for a Christian that we are to encourage, motivate, praise, and love one another in doing and into doing good works. We are always to be with one another with excitement and joy, as we know we are a holy body of one where our ultimate destination is coming closer each day to the return of Jesus Christ.

The scripture we will visit in our conclusion will be Colossians 3:16:

Let the word of Christ dwell in you richly, teaching and admonishing one another in all wisdom, singing psalms and hymns and spiritual songs, with thankfulness in your hearts to God.

What an amazing verse in this love story! We are to absorb the love of Christ in us completely and through one another in our words and actions while we share, grow, and praise the Almighty, knowing how blessed we are to be His children together.

As a final thought: we as Christians are supposed to do as God's Word commands. We have learned what a blessing it is to become who God intends us to be when we are one in unity together as His children. Find others, make it your mission that they know they are loved, and bring them to your flock so that they know there is a place where they are supposed to be and that God is waiting for them.

One of the most important commitments you can make as a Christian is to read your Bible every day. In each message, we will provide you with a few scriptures to look up and read on your own to plant seeds inside of you for a deeper understanding so you can grow closer to Jesus Christ through His written word.

It's time to get your Bible. For your growing with God, scriptures for the message "Birds of a Feather Flock Together" are Ecclesiastes 4:9–12, Acts 2:44–47, John 17:21–23.

I pray that this message creates a path for you to grow closer to Jesus Christ or meet Him for the first time. If you want to receive the guaranteed passage that He sacrificed Himself on the cross for so you can be saved as a child of God, then become who you are created to be and turn the words you read in this book into action now so you can have eternal life in the kingdom of heaven that is just waiting for you.

Planting Notes:

_____

_____

_____

_____

_____

Can You Be Parented?

Have you ever known a child who just would not mind instruction no matter what was done? It seems that the child is disciplined all the time. Or have you ever known a child who behaves perfectly all the time? It seems that the child is constantly blessed and full of joy. Do you know what type of a child of God you are?

In this message, we are going to explore whether you can be parented or not. Do you even know if you can? It is kind of a funny question to ponder, but the reality is God is the Father and you are His child when you are born again. So, you must be of the mindset that you will be parented, and you should want to be parented so that you know God is always there for you and loves you. Plus, it gives God a guarantee you will be in the kingdom with Him through your obedience to His Word.

Let's begin with a few questions you need to ask yourself to know if you can be parented or if you need to change to have your best life with God now. Do you have issues with authority? Do you not like following instructions and want to do things your own way? Do you have a rebellious and defiant personality? Do you always have to be the center of attention? Are you stubborn and not open to change? Are you not willing to listen to advice from others with wisdom?

Do you not respect the advice and opinions of others that try to make your life better? Are you rude to others when they are offering you guidance? Do you have an overaggressive spirit? Do you find yourself angry and frustrated all the time? Do you lash out at others for no reason because you are really upset with yourself? Do you constantly argue or debate others just because you want your opinion to be heard? Do you think you know everything? Are you arrogant and prideful?

If you answered yes to any of these questions, there is a good chance you cannot or refuse to be parented. So, wait a minute! Listen up: if you absolutely will not be parented, then how do you expect to have a holy relationship with God the Father as His child?

How will you follow the guidance of Jesus Christ to be saved? The reality is that you won't if you can't be parented; there is no way to have a relationship with Jesus and God the Father to be saved when you refuse to follow His Word, direction, and correction.

So by now, you have come to realize that refusing to be parented is a sin. Refusing to be parented by your own parents or by God is a one-way ticket to nowhere except a bath of eternal fire. Every time you refuse to listen and follow what is done for you out of love, you walk further away from God until He can't see or hear you anymore.

Keep in mind: the verses in Scripture that apply to our obedience to follow parenting aren't always obvious. Just because a verse doesn't say "mothers" or "fathers" doesn't mean it doesn't apply. As a parent, you take on many roles: leader, teacher, counselor, mentor, pastor, and many more. Parenting can come from God through others He uses to instruct what He wants of you.

It is important to realize that when Scripture speaks a word to teachers and leaders or even just to all people, it applies to your parenting role, too. For example, when Jesus says, "love one another as I have loved you" (John 13:34, paraphrased), there are no exceptions within this word you are to follow. As a parent, you are told to love your children as Jesus loves you. Because you are a child of God, you will be parented with love for you to ensure your path will bring you home where He has already prepared a place for you.

Children are always to obey their parents and the Word of God because they belong to the Lord and it is the right thing to do.

> "Honor your father and mother." This is the first commandment with a promise: If you honor your father and

mother, "Things will go well for you, and you will have a long life on the earth."

Ephesians 6:2–3 (NLT)

So we can clearly determine if we do not follow the guidance as a child of God and honor those who bring wisdom to us, we can expect discipline and correction to be the choice we have made out of rebellion.

We will now explore the scripture of Deuteronomy 21:18–21:

> If a man has a stubborn and rebellious son who will not obey the voice of his father or the voice of his mother, and, though they discipline him, will not listen to them, then his father and his mother shall take hold of him and bring him out to the elders of his city at the gate of the place where he lives, and they shall say to the elders of his city, "This our son is stubborn and rebellious; he will not obey our voice; he is a glutton and a drunkard." Then all the men of the city shall stone him to death with stones. So you shall purge the evil from your midst, and all Israel shall hear, and fear.

This scripture clearly represents how serious God is about you being parented and following His Word and guidance. In the world of today, you see this happen every day when a child becomes so out of control they are consumed with the evil of the world. So, just as the Scriptures say, they will be sent out to the world to suffer, which will lead them only to death because they refused to be parented.

As we can see, this next scripture validates the definite position of consequence you can expect from not following the instruction by God of being parented through wisdom:

> For rebellion is as the sin of divination, and presumption is as iniquity and idolatry. Because you have rejected the word of the LORD, he has also rejected you from being a king.

1 Samuel 15:23

As a final thought: the willingness to be parented is directly related to being saved through Jesus Christ and your best relationship with God. Parenting comes in all forms, from all kinds of people, and is in His written word, in spoken word, in actions that surround all areas of your life that God wants you to learn wisdom from so you can grow as His child. You must always be open to taking one step closer to God by listening and following all the ways He may lead you on your path home.

One of the most important commitments you can make as a Christian is to read your Bible every day. In each message, we will provide you with a few scriptures to look up and read on your own to plant seeds inside of you for a deeper understanding so you can grow closer to Jesus Christ through His written word.

It's time to get your Bible. For your growing with God, scriptures for the message "Can You Be Parented?" are Proverbs 22:6, Psalm 103:13, and Exodus 20:12.

I pray that this message creates a path for you to grow closer to Jesus Christ or meet Him for the first time. If you want to receive the guaranteed passage that He sacrificed Himself on the cross for so you can be saved as a child of God, then become who you are created to be and turn the words you read in this book into action now so you can have eternal life in the kingdom of heaven that is just waiting for you.

Planting Notes:

_____

_____

_____

_____

_____

Do You Need an Eye Exam?

If you could see what other people are looking at through their eyes, you would be so shocked at what even some of the closest people you know are viewing with their eyes. The eyes are the food source for the mind, and the mind affects your entire physical and emotional body and life.

Let's get started! So, the questions are: Do you need an eye exam? Is your vision blurry? Are you getting lost because you can't read clear directions? Are you seeing things that you are not supposed to be seeing? Do you know the eyes are the gateway to the soul? Whatever the eyes see, good or bad, the soul will process and make it a part of you, who you are, and the direction your life will end up.

Don't you think there was a reason God wanted you to see what was happening to Jesus? He could have just made Him disappear into thin air! But He didn't, for a reason. We as humans believe what we see more than what we hear. This is why we were witnessing the sacrifice of Jesus Christ on the cross visually. What was seen by the eyes of many was so powerful when Jesus Christ was crucified that we still see those images in today's world with our own eyes.

So, have you ever heard the saying "I will believe it when I see it"? Well, why do you think Jesus did so many miracles? To make us believe by what we saw with our eyes, as He knew that was the way to our soul. It is what determines the direction you go in your life. It is your internal processor. Your eyes can bless or fool you and lead you to destruction or heaven. It just depends on what you allow them to see.

You are what your environments are, and your eyes lead you to those places. So you must pay very close attention to what you allow your eyes to witness in your walk with God.

When people see the light of God in your soul, it is usually through your eyes. So you may need an eye exam regularly just to make sure your vision is clear and you are seeing what your eyes were meant to see with the gift of sight from God.

Let's do a quick self eye exam. Do you read your Bible? Do you attend church? Do you fellowship? Do you do good works? Do you put others in front of you? Do you watch things on TV that are ungodly? Do you have any type of addiction like pornography? Do you watch shows that promote crime and evil on TV or at the movies?

Suppose you were given a choice of two ways to go in the same direction you want to go. Are you going to walk down a pitch-black scary dark alley where anyone can pop out on you anywhere because you can't see in the dark or a safe, lighted path where other people are around? Which one would you choose and why?

It all has to do with your sight of what you see that should automatically tell you if where you are heading is the direction God would send you or is where Satan would like to see you go. Satan's whole purpose is to get you to walk over to the dark side and never let you see the light again. So you now understand where your eyes go, you will always follow.

What should you do? Always keep your eyes focused on where Jesus would have His and nowhere else. Always look up and look away at things you know you should not feed your mind with or be looking at. Remember that is a sin. Listen: if you are a Christian, you absolutely know what is wrong and right. You know when you view things that steal your relationship with God, how dirty and ashamed it makes you feel. Focus your eyes on Jesus and the Word of God in everything you look at with your eyes that feed your soul.

Now let's look at some scriptures in regard to what the Bible says about what you see with your eyes. We will start with the verse of Matthew 5:29: "If your right eye causes you to sin, tear it out and throw it away. For it is better that you lose one of your members than that your whole body be thrown into hell."

God feels so strongly about what you view with your eyes is always holy and godly that He would rather you remove one of your eyes that have sinned in order to save you from the other one, causing your death and bypassing eternal life with Him.

Now let's look at the scripture of Proverbs 21:4: "Haughty eyes and a proud heart, the lamp of the wicked, are sin." We can plainly see that if you focus on what you look at and that is sin, then you are serving the host of evil and following the path of darkness in your heart while you are destroying your relationship with Jesus.

The scripture we will conclude this message with is Psalm 38:10: "My heart throbs; my strength fails me, and the light of my eyes—it also has gone from me." It is very simple to understand this verse. Suppose you choose to focus on what you see with your eyes: on the ways of the world and sin. Everything that you are with God in you will vanish and be removed from you by your own doing.

As a final thought: you should always be looking up, and you should know what is godly and evil just by sight, with your eyes. The choice is yours in regard to what you choose to see with your eyes. You will either see Satan in hell or God in heaven. I pray that you are with me, walking with Jesus in the kingdom of heaven.

One of the most important commitments you can make as a Christian is to read your Bible every day. In each message, we will provide you with a few scriptures to look up and read on your own to plant seeds inside of you for a deeper understanding so you can grow closer to Jesus Christ through His written word.

It's time to get your Bible. For your growing with God, scriptures for the message "Do You Need an Eye Exam?" are Psalm 119:37, Matthew 7:3, Psalm 101:3.

I pray that this message creates a path for you to grow closer to Jesus Christ or meet Him for the first time. If you want to receive the guaranteed passage that He sacrificed Himself on the cross for so you can be saved as a child of God, then become who you are created to be and turn the words you read in this book into action now so you can have eternal life in the kingdom of heaven that is just waiting for you.

Planting Notes:

_____

_____

_____

_____

_____

The Puddle of Patience

Everyone, no matter who he or she is, needs to learn more patience. In today's crazy world, there occur so many unexpected events that can just frustrate us beyond belief. It is as if everything needs to be on "go!" "go!" "go!" twenty-four hours a day, seven days a week, just pushing our ability to stay in grace with patience.

Let's talk about what a puddle is. A puddle is the still perfection of living water with the extreme reflection of clarity. It maintains who it is even during a storm as raindrops cause ripples and waves, and the puddle even grows from experiencing those ripples and waves. It can see through anyone that looks into it. Through all of this, the puddle remains totally patient and silent in its stillness without the limit of time, just as your patience should be as a child of God.

Just as Jesus said: "You do not realize now what I am doing, but later you will understand" (John 13:7, NIV). "Be completely humble and gentle; be patient, bearing with one another in love" (Ephesians 4:2, NIV).

Let's explore Psalm 37:7–9:

> Be still before the Lord and wait patiently for him; fret not yourself over the one who prospers in his way, over the man who carries out evil devices! Refrain from anger, and forsake wrath! Fret not yourself; it tends only to evil. For the evildoers shall be cut off, but those who wait patiently for the Lord shall inherit the kingdom.

Follow along and don't miss this as we unlock the blessings of God's written word in this Psalms verse for a clear understanding:

"Be still": you are to take place, occur, be involved, or participate and not to move or make a sound but only exist in perfect silence.

"Before the Lord": you are in front of the Lord and Savior.

"And wait patiently for him": you are to connect or join to and stay where you are for an indefinite period of time in a way that shows tolerance of delays, problems, or suffering without becoming annoyed or anxious with excited expectations for the Lord's arrival, sharing His plan with you for the direction of your life as His child.

"Fret not yourself": do not be constantly or visibly worried or anxious in a state of anxiety so you can exclude yourself personally from those chains of burden.

"Over the one who prospers in his way": you are expressing authority or control over your emotions being directed based on the action of a person. It is a generalized reference of one as opposed to many or none in regard to the person who succeeds in material terms and is financially successful. This is an impression of a situation or something that is or appears to be belonging to or associated with one's characteristic or habitual manner of behavior based on your perception.

"Over the man who carries out evil devices": you are expressing authority or control over your emotions being directed based on the action of a person. It is a generalized reference of one as opposed to many or none at all.

"Refrain from anger": you are to stop yourself from doing something where potential harm or regret exists that indicates the point in space at which a journey, emotion, or action starts to become a strong feeling of annoyance, negativity, displeasure, or hostility.

"And forsake wrath": you are to connect or join in renouncing, giving up, and abandoning the temptation of evil or perpetuating the action of extreme anger.

"Fret not yourself": do not be constantly or visibly worried or anxious, in a state of anxiety or worry, and exclude yourself personally from the chains of burden.

"It tends only to evil": this is the action of denoting a person or thing that regularly or frequently behaves in a particular way, solely or exclusively expressing motion in the direction of the profoundly immoral and wickedness, embodying or associated with the forces of the devil.

"For the evildoers shall be cut off": this is to indicate the place someone or something is going toward, denoting one or more people or things who commit profoundly immoral and malevolent deeds. They express a strong assertion or intention for you to take place with them, occur, be involved, participate, or be divided so as to be removed or separated from your moral values and beliefs as a Christian.

"But those who wait patiently for the Lord": this is used to introduce a response expressing a feeling used to identify a specific person or thing, a person who stays where you are for an indefinite period of time in a way that shows tolerance of delays, problems, or suffering without becoming annoyed or anxious with excited expectations in anticipation of God or Jesus Christ.

"Shall inherit the kingdom": this expresses a strong assertion or intention of future events to come into possession of someone as a right, denoting that one or more people embrace the spiritual reign or authority of God, the rule of God or Jesus Christ in a future age in heaven as the place of God and of the faithful after physical death.

May your understanding and clarity of these blessings in Psalm 37:7–9 bring you a greater knowledge of how to become who God intends you to be!

One of the most important commitments you can make as a Christian is to read your Bible every day. In each message, we will provide you with a few scriptures to look up and read on your own

to plant seeds inside of you for a deeper understanding so you can grow closer to Jesus Christ through His written word.

It's time to get your Bible. For your growing with God, scriptures for the message "The Puddle of Patience" are Romans 12:12, Romans 8:25, and Ephesians 4:2.

I pray that this message creates a path for you to grow closer to Jesus Christ or meet Him for the first time. If you want to receive the guaranteed passage that He sacrificed Himself on the cross for so you can be saved as a child of God, then become who you are created to be and turn the words you read in this book into action now so you can have eternal life in the kingdom of heaven that is just waiting for you.

Planting Notes:

_____

_____

_____

_____

_____

How Do I Know I Am Saved?

Have you ever declared to Jesus Christ that you want to be saved and be born new again? What happens then? Do you know? Once you are saved by Christ through repentance and salvation, you are always saved. But really, how do you know for sure God knows you?

How does being saved through Jesus Christ really work? It is one of the most important questions a Christian struggles with and gets very confused about. We know from His Word salvation is not based on your good works. Christians can feel, at times, unsure that they are saved. It is often your faith weakening, allowing the seed of doubt to be planted into your mind. Some people tend to feel like they are not "good enough" or worthy of being saved by God.

Maybe your faith is not true, and you have moments of weakness that can steal your joy and assurance of being saved by God that has always been there for you. You may think, *Is there a way of knowing if I am saved or not? Is it normal to feel unsure? Am I failing God if I feel this way?*

When we're tossed about as if we are living in a storm of uncertainty, it's almost impossible for us to progress in our Christian life. God is a God of peace, not doubt or confusion, so know that if these emotions arise in you, they are not from God. It is the daily battle occurring over you as a child of God.

But the most amazing thing is we don't have to be unsure and let Satan seed our minds with doubt and whatever else he can to distract us from living by the Word of the Lord and Savior. God provides clear ways for us to have the full assurance of salvation.

Scripture testifies that receiving salvation from the penalty of sin is made possible by your faith in the works of Jesus Christ, who atoned for your sins by His death on the cross in place of you. God's only requirement for full payment of your sins was His only Son, Jesus Christ, who paid by being crucified on the cross.

So what does this mean? It means that not one person's works play any part in their salvation. We can do nothing more to add to the perfection of the accomplishments of Christ on the cross. With that being said, it is made clear that only by faith in His work may we be saved.

Let's look at the first way we know we're saved, which is that the Bible says so. There is no other book in existence or ever will be that is like the Bible, and it is God speaking His word directly to you. We know with full assurance that God does not lie, so we can absolutely believe, trust, and rely on His Word that navigates our life and destiny as His children.

Let's explore Scripture with John 5:13 (NLT) that says this: "I have written this to you who believe in the name of the Son of God that you may know that you have eternal life."

This verse shows us God doesn't want us to be unsure about our salvation. We have something in writing—the Word of God—by which we can *know* we're really saved. God wants us to be assured of our salvation by His written word that never changes and will forever remain.

If you believe that Jesus is the Lord, the Son of God, and that His death and resurrection are proof of His claims, then you are saved. The Word of God leaves no doubt or question concerning this outcome. The moment of your faith is the moment of your salvation…by faith, you have already been saved!

The next way we know we are saved is the Holy Spirit witnesses with our spirit, meaning that we as His children are vessels delivering the Word of God with Him and Him through us.

The absolute proof that you are saved is through the Spirit of God. He gave us two gifts for eternal life. Do you know what they are? The Bible is the first, which is something outside of us, as it is a spiritual declaration of the Word of God, and His Spirit, which lives inside all of His children, and we are the physical declaration of the Word of God. Both testify that when we believe in Jesus, then we are saved eternally with the Father and the Son.

Let's hear what Scripture tells us about us being born again by believing in Jesus and the Spirit coming into our spirit to live in us forever. Romans 8:16 speaks clearly concerning these two spirits: "The Spirit Himself bears witness with our spirit that we are children of God."

One reason we may wonder whether we're saved may be because we don't know how to experience witnessing of the Holy Spirit within our spirit. Instead, we may rely on our confusing feelings or our doubting mind to assure us we're saved.

But the key to witnessing the Holy Spirit is to realize that within our heart is the spirit of God, which is a deeper relationship with God than our thoughts in our mind have, which think of the Holy Spirit and can go in conjunction with the spirit and the heart, but the true Holy Spirit comes from having a heart of God. The key is bringing the spirit of the heart and the mind together, and that is only done through reading, knowing, and living by the Word of God.

It means that your heart is far deeper in your spirit with God than your mind is. As God's spirit is in your heart, and your heart is what you feel with, and that is how the spirit of God works within us.

On the other hand, our minds have the potential to allow things that are not of God to enter them. This is why you do not *think* the spirit of God; you *feel* the spirit of God as His child, as His desire is to be in your heart. Where the heart goes, the mind follows.

So, if you are concerned about not being saved, rest assured that such doubts and feelings are normal for Christians and are not of God. The enemy delights in bringing doubts to our minds and causing us to wonder if we are "good enough."

The true reality is that none of us is good enough to be saved! We never were. We don't deserve the salvation we have received, and we can never allow ourselves to think that we do "deserve" God's grace. Grace, by definition, is not deserved or earned but only given through salvation.

As we are nearing the conclusion of this message, we must realize another way we know that we are saved is by the *love* for our brothers and sisters in the Lord. In addition to the Word of God and the Spirit in us, we can know we're saved because we have a genuine love for our fellow Christians, even for those who may be very different from ourselves and regardless of where their walk with Jesus is at that moment because you will always love them as God loves you.

This love we receive from God isn't something we had before we were saved, and it's not something we manufacture after we're saved. It's the spontaneous result of our receiving the life of God as His children. Let's look at Scripture for further instruction. In 1 John 3:14, the apostle John says, "We know that we have passed out of death into life because we love the brothers."

Always remember that your faith in the Lord is the way to know you are saved and for you to pass death by and into eternal life, and the love toward the brothers and sisters is the evidence that you have passed death by and into eternal life. To have faith is to receive the eternal life; to love is to live by the eternal life with the Father and the Son and express it to others. This love in us for our brothers and sisters in the Lord is further evidence that we're genuinely saved as His children.

In conclusion, your faith is a gift of God. It did not depend on our own resolve or determination to believe. The Bible says our belief is a gift from God, as Paul explains: "For by grace you have been saved through faith; and that not of yourselves, it is the gift of God" (Ephesians 2:8).

One of the most important commitments you can make as a Christian is to read your Bible every day. In each message, we will provide you with a few scriptures to look up and read on your own to plant seeds inside of you for a deeper understanding so you can grow closer to Jesus Christ through His written word.

It's time to get your Bible. For your growing with God, scriptures for the message "How Do I Know I Am Saved?" are Ephesians 2:8–9, Acts 2:38, and 1 John 5:13.

I pray that this message creates a path for you to grow closer to Jesus Christ or meet Him for the first time. If you want to receive the guaranteed passage that He sacrificed Himself on the cross for so you can be saved as a child of God, then become who you are created to be and turn the words you read in this book into action now so you can have eternal life in the kingdom of heaven that is just waiting for you.

Planting Notes:

_____

_____

_____

_____

_____

Unity in Christ

When we look back through history at all the major conflicts of humanity, we see it all started with the lack of unity and the existing separation creating conflict. People act in a way that they were not created for, therefore, reacting to the dark side of Satan's temptation and destruction.

What is unity? What does unity mean? Why do I need to know what God says about unity? Let's get on the subject of unity that is on everyone's minds. What is the purpose of unity? Why does God command unity among His people in the Bible? What happens if we do not follow His command of unity? How does unity affect your life and salvation? What is one of the most powerful moments of unity that ever existed?

One thing you need to understand is that God directs and allows all things to occur for reasons we do not understand that contain a message or a result He desires from you or for you. There could have been any man chosen to help Jesus carry the burden of the cross. But when Jesus fell after being brutalized and tortured, God sent a man who was chosen to help Jesus complete His sacrifice on the cross. Even though the Romans told this man to do so, do not think for one minute that it was not a directive from God, as you will learn the man was unknowingly becoming part of the most amazing events the world has ever seen by helping Jesus Christ complete God's commandments of His Son's sacrifice to pay the debt for the sins of all of us for eternity.

The man who the Romans ordered to help Jesus carry the cross did not know how important He was and what He represented. This man was now a part of the most important occurrence in biblical history that has or will ever happen.

God could have chosen any man and directed it to be done through the enemies of Jesus, but He chose the one that represented unity as a part of the sacrifice and death of His Son that will change the world forever. So you will never forget God chose someone completely different from Jesus to help His Son walk the last steps to His death on the cross.

Who was the man who helped Jesus carry the cross? Matthew, Mark, and Luke all identify the man who helped Jesus carry the cross as Simon, a man from Cyrene. Due to this action, Simon became a follower of Jesus. Simon knew what he did for Him was in no comparison to the sacrifice Jesus made for him. We can see why Simon of Cyrene is now a major part of biblical history, helping Jesus carry the cross to His death.

Cyrene was an ancient city in Libya, Africa. Its location has led to many traditional depictions of Simon as an African black man.

There is speculation based on some church tradition that Simon of Cyrene later became a Christian—some theories state that he was already a follower of Christ before the crucifixion—and was a leader in the early church. This may be why God sent him through the Romans to help His Son on the cross.

Well, we saw an amazing example of one of the greatest moments of unity that ever existed. You must understand it is His Word and commandment that we all are in a race and to love one another as He loves all of us. He will accept nothing less if we want to enter the kingdom of heaven.

Let us look at yet another incredible example of unity in Christ. This is another of the many messages of unity that occurred during the final moments of the life of Jesus Christ. It was when one of the criminals who were hanged blasphemed Him, saying, "If You are Christ, save Yourself and us." But the other, answering, rebuked him, saying, "Do you not even fear God, seeing you are under the same condemnation? And we indeed justly, for we receive the due reward of our deeds; but this Man has done nothing wrong." Then he said to Jesus, "Lord, remember me when You come into Your kingdom." And Jesus said to him, "Assuredly, I say to you, today you will be with Me in paradise."

Luke 23:39–43 (NKJV)

Do you realize this is another example of unity in Christ? Jesus welcomed a sinner being put to death next to Him to paradise with Him for believing in who He was after a life of serving evil.

This action very loudly states the kingdom of heaven is for everyone, as we are all one in the eyes of the Lord. We are unified as His children and are all made in His image. All He wants is that you repent of your sins, asking to be forgiven and saved and accept Him as your Lord and Savior. What greater example of unity can exist than to bring the one who has sinned against you to be forgiven and enter your house with forgiveness and eternal life with the Father, the Son, and the Holy Spirit in the kingdom of heaven?

Let us look at the most powerful example of unity in Christ that Jesus showed us, dying on the cross. With His final breath, He said, "Father, forgive them, for they know not what they do" (Luke 23:34). As He was dying, Jesus was pleading with God to save our souls that they may become perfectly one, unified, in *unity*. And you better believe God expects His commandments to be kept since He gave His Son's life for you. We all must love one another exactly how Jesus loves us.

One of the most important commitments you can make as a Christian is to read your Bible every day. In each message, we will provide you with a few scriptures to look up and read on your own to plant seeds inside of you for a deeper understanding so you can grow closer to Jesus Christ through His written word.

It's time to get your Bible. For your growing with God, scriptures for the message "Unity in Christ" are Corinthians 1:10, Philippians 2:2, and Romans 15:15.

I pray that this message creates a path for you to grow closer to Jesus Christ or meet Him for the first time. If you want to receive the guaranteed passage that He sacrificed Himself on the cross for so you can be saved as a child of God, then become who you are created to be and turn the words you read in this book into action now so you can have eternal life in the kingdom of heaven that is just waiting for you.

Planting Notes:

_____

_____

_____

_____

_____

Walk like a Christian

Christians come in all shapes, sizes, and personalities, but you can usually spot a real person of faith fairly easily because you see God in them. They always seem to carry themselves differently than others. Have you ever wondered why a Christian is the way they are as a person?

We know from the Bible that a genuine Christian has repented of their sins and trusts in Christ alone for salvation. When this happens, we are made into a new creation. So what does this new creation actually look like? How does this person act? What signs show that he or she is a new creation and not just a false convert?

There are many hurdles that are put in your way of walking like a Christian. Is the world still causing you to suffer after you are reborn? Is your life different after you are born new again in Christ? Are you still affected by the world in the way you were before you were saved? Do you act and react differently to any situation in your life? Do you allow stress or faith to guide your life? Do you know what peace is? Have you experienced joy? Are you supposed to act and appear completely different as a Christian? Are you walking daily with God now or just coming by for visits?

How do you know when you are where God wants you to be? He lets you know by how He teaches you in your life with love as His child. The first and most important step in walking like a Christian to be where God wants you to be is obedience. Obedience to the Word and all that it is and will ever be.

This book of simple instructions, once followed, puts you in a place where the world no longer affects who you are and how you feel. It may affect what you do but only to what God sees fit to be allowed. It is no longer a place of burden, worry, and stress as long as you walk in the footsteps of faith and know that God will provide and be there for you always.

Suppose you have committed yourself and accepted the full transformation as a child of God. Nothing in your life should be the same after you are saved. The way you think and act should be completely different. The world will still be there, and you may not like how it affects you, but it is not your concern.

God will take care of your needs based on you exactly following His Word. There are specific behaviors a Christian has that should be a permanent part of you in your walk with God.

Follow the example and teachings of Jesus Christ contained in the holy Bible. It's the only *real* how-to or DIY book about exactly how to be a Christian! Seek the baptism of the Holy Spirit because it is a promise given to everybody as an announcement of your belief and faith in Jesus Christ.

There are several steps in your walk as a Christian. We will explore the behavior that you must have, and that is to *love* God above all else, even to the point of becoming selfless so that you can give to others. There is nothing about Jesus Christ that is selfish. He gave everything to everyone all the time. The next behavior step that should become part of who you are as a Christian is to have undying faith and never allow the sin of doubt to poison your walk with God.

As we continue down the path in our walk as Christians, we must also *love others* as Christ loves us. That includes people you may not like or get along with. They probably have not met Jesus yet, and you may be that example that brings others to meet Him. Do not hate; it is a sin and feeds Satan's desires to destroy you.

Moving on to the next step: to always do good in anything that you do, not to have a bigger treasure in heaven but because you want to do a good/right thing for yourself and others.

You glorify God every time you do a good deed or perform an act of kindness since you are one of His children.

Keep in mind that small acts of goodness can make big changes in others' lives. We are supposed to do as Jesus did all the way to the cross. As a Christian, you should always be looking for opportunities to show others the way to find Jesus. You will be given a choice to help others as someone did for you if you are walking as a Christian should.

In our next step, we look at one of the greatest challenges to walk as a Christian: not to judge others. Many people have trouble with that one because we are bombarded by images every single day that tell us we are all different all the time and we are to judge others that way when, in reality, we are all the same. Judging is for God to do, not us. As Christians, we are called to love each other, and that means leaving the judging to God.

One of the most important steps to walk like a Christian is to read your Bible and pray every day, just like eating and drinking to sustain your soul and body. You should start your day and end it in prayer with God. If something occurs that you need God, then just find a place and call out to Him in prayer. He is there every minute of every day and night.

Next is you must always keep on giving God your *all* in your steps of faith as you walk like a Christian. That means to give up your right to sin in any manner willfully. Remember to repent, which means you see the wrong you're doing and you quit doing it and ask for forgiveness and guidance.

Share with everyone you meet and know the message of Jesus Christ and be constantly reminded where God brought you from and where you are now. That will help you spread the Word of God. Jesus died for all of us, and the only way others can hear is to tell them. Always be a blessing to others.

Not sure how to bring up Jesus? One question works every time. Just say to someone, "I have a question someone asked me, and I wanted to see what your thoughts were. If you died today, are you sure you would go to heaven?"

Now let's explore Scripture about walking like a Christian. Many of us are very familiar with the first two verses of Romans 12:

> I beseech you therefore, brethren, by the mercies of God, that you present your bodies a living sacrifice, holy, acceptable to God, which is your reasonable service. And do not be conformed to this world, but be transformed by the renewing of your mind, that you may prove what is good and acceptable and the perfect will of God.
>
> Romans 12:1–2 (NKJV)

As a final thought to this message: let's remember one very important thing. The Christian life is not—and never will be—about perfection. None of us will ever be the "perfect Christian." Our focus must not be on being perfect but on testing our heart's desire and our direction to ensure we are where God wants us. What direction are we going? Are we growing in these things each year? Do we look more like Christ as we mature in the faith? What is our attitude to these things?

All of us will struggle, and some will more than others. And that's okay, too. If we know there is a battle, then we know the Holy Spirit is hard at work, convicting us and showing us how we can grow. Walking as a Christian every day is the pursuit of perfection, as we are made in His image, but there is only one God the Father, God the Son, and God the Holy Spirit.

One of the most important commitments you can make as a Christian is to read your Bible every day. In each message, we will provide you with a few scriptures to look up and read on your own to plant seeds inside of you for a deeper understanding so you can grow closer to Jesus Christ through His written word.

It's time to get your Bible. For your growing with God, scriptures for the message "Walk like a Christian" are Corinthians 5:17, 1 John 2:6, and Romans 8:4.

I pray that this message creates a path for you to grow closer to Jesus Christ or meet Him for the first time. If you want to receive the guaranteed passage that He sacrificed Himself on the cross for so you can be saved as a child of God, then become who you are created to be and turn the words you read in this book into action now so you can have eternal life in the kingdom of heaven that is just waiting for you.

Planting Notes:

_____

_____

_____

_____

_____

What Are Your Priorities in Life Based on Scripture?

Priorities in our life begin at birth and change as we get older. If you are a newborn baby, you usually have about three priorities: to eat, poop, and sleep, and as you grow, they constantly become different. The amazing thing is priorities are sometimes done for us, like breathing, but mostly, we set our own rules to follow based on the decisions we make about what is the most important thing in our lives.

Do your relationship priorities matter in following the Word of God? You better believe they do. Although there really is no written order, for a child of God, the Scriptures are pretty clear. When we look, we can easily find scriptures and God's word for our relationship priorities.

We are going to explore several verses of Scripture during this chapter, exploring message seven relationship priorities in life based on Scripture. First, let's briefly share what the seven priorities are, and then the message will expose the correct order Scripture expects us to follow and why God has committed His Word to these priorities. The seven relationship priorities in life are the following: God, marriage, children, parents, extended family, fellow believers, and the world itself. The order and manner you follow these will determine your obedience to the instructions in God's Word.

It is pretty obvious that God comes first: "Love the LORD your God with all your heart and with all your soul and with all your strength"

(Deuteronomy 6:5, NIV). All of one's heart, soul, and strength is to be committed to loving God, making Him the first priority.

One definite way to show God is first in your life is by belonging to a church and attending regularly. It is not just being there but being a part of the body of the church by fellowshipping and encouraging one another in Christ. "Not giving up meeting together, as some are in the habit of doing, but encouraging one another—and all the more as you see the Day approaching" (Hebrews 10:25, NIV).

If you are married, then your spouse comes next. "Husbands, love your wives, just as Christ loved the church and gave himself up for her" (Ephesians 5:25, NIV). Now let's expand on that so we have a better understanding.

As a married man, you are to love your wife without limits. Give your life to her, respect and honor her, cherish her as if she was your creation, as this is how God loves the church and you are to love your wife, as you are one flesh. As you are one flesh with her, know that if you bring any ungodly behavior or action in your marriage to her, you also bring it upon yourself the very same second. God is your first priority, but she is to receive the same reverence that the Lord does.

So we have discovered so far that Christ is the first priority, then after obeying and glorifying the Father and becoming a part of the body of the church, your wife. In the same way, wives are to be devoted to their husbands "as to the Lord." The husband is to receive the same reverence as the Lord, just as the wives, as they are both second to God in your life-relationship priorities.

We know now that husbands and wives are second-only-to-God priorities in life, and since a husband and wife are one flesh, "For this reason a man will leave his father and mother and be united to his wife, and the two will become one flesh" (Ephesians 5:31, NIV). So it stands to reason that the result of the marriage relationship would be children, and they should be the next priority.

Parents are to raise godly children who will be the next generation of those who love the Lord with all their hearts. "Start children off on the way they should go, and even when they are old they will not turn from it" (Proverbs 22:6, NIV). "Fathers, do not exasperate your children; instead, bring them up in the training and instruction of the Lord" (Ephesians 6:4, NIV).

Do not create a confrontation with your children but love them with direction and correction unto God's Word always as He does you. All of your other family relationships should reflect the same values and principles, and everyone you have any type of relationship with in your life should be communicated with on godly principles. This shows once again that God comes first.

Now, the last part of this message will be about our parents.

> Honor your father and your mother, as the LORD your God has commanded you, so that you may live long and that it may go well with you in the land the LORD your God is giving you.
>
> Deuteronomy 5:16 (NIV)

This tells us to honor our parents so that we may live long and that things will go well with us. There is no age limit specified to where we do not honor or value our parents or not include them in our lives, which leads us to believe that as long as our parents are alive, we should honor them. Of course, once a child reaches adulthood, he or she is no longer obligated to obey them, but there is no age limit to honoring them.

This is so very important in today's world that you cherish and honor your parents that gave you life through a miracle from God. Do not buy into the world's view that friends are more important than anything. Avoid the ignorance and evil intentions of the world to destroy God's family, as they try to remove family from every holiday or even just spending time together in church or just honoring them by spending time with them. You should love them as God loves you, and they are a priority in your life.

We can conclude from this that parents are next in the list of priorities after God, our spouses, and our children. So we have concluded the first four priorities in your relationships in life should be God first, your marriage, then your children, and then your parents.

After parents comes the rest of one's family, which we will visit in part two. "But those who won't care for their relatives, especially those in their own household, have denied the true faith" (1 Timothy 5:8, NLT).

We have completed the first four life-relationship priorities with our parents. Can you tell what the first four life-relationship priorities from the part one message are without assistance? Well, let's review what we have learned so far. Our first life-relationship priorities are: God, number one always, your marriage and spouse are number two, your children are number three, and your parents are number four.

After parents comes the rest of one's family, which is your extended family. We will start with 1 Timothy 5:8 (NLT): "But those who won't care for their relatives, especially those in their own household, have denied the true faith. Such people are worse than unbelievers."

Did you catch that? God's instruction is so defined about how you are to care for your extended family and relatives that you are looked at as an unbeliever if you act in any other way toward your extended family or relatives. Our biggest challenge with extended family is being able to connect with them as we do with our immediate family and share the love for Jesus with them the same way as with your immediate family.

Even though it may take a little more effort to reach them, it is nothing compared to what Jesus did to reach all of us through His sacrifice to save all of us, which we did not deserve.

Jesus did not care whether it was immediate family, extended family, parents, fellow believers, or those He did not even know. Jesus's sacrifice was to save everyone and love them all equally, and they are all children of God. This is the same way you should care for your extended family and relatives, as it shows that you are placing God first in your priorities and becoming who He intends you to be. So, now we know extended family and relatives and number five in your life-relationship priorities.

Next in our list of priorities are our extended family and then other Christians. As a believer, you are also never to create circumstances where you judge, treat differently, or cause your brothers or sisters to damage their relationship with Jesus.

It is important to recognize that there are many encouragements in 1 Corinthians from Paul on how all followers of Christ should live and the church should instruct. We are to love each other, serve each other, and remain in harmony through unity as children of God.

There are many scriptural verses stating unity in God's Word for all of His children.

"Only do not use your freedom as an opportunity for the flesh, but through love serve one another" (Galatians 5:13). "Be kind and compassionate to one another, forgiving each other, just as in Christ God forgave you" (Ephesians 4:32, NIV). "Encourage one another and build each other up" (1 Thessalonians 5:11, NIV). "Consider how we may spur one another on toward love and good deeds" (Hebrews 10:24, NIV).

Finally, in our life priorities comes the rest of the world. The priority of all in the world is very simple: "Therefore go and make disciples of all nations, baptizing them in the name of the Father and of the Son and of the Holy Spirit" (Matthew 28:19, NIV).

The world exists for God's creation to be saved, and that is the only purpose of its priority. God created the world and then had to sacrifice His only Son, Jesus Christ, on the cross to save all of His children and guarantee a way to the Father through the Son for those who not only believe in Him but follow His Word and live their life, honoring our Lord and Savior, based on how they choose their life-relationship priorities.

In conclusion, the scriptural order of life-relationships priorities is: God first in everything, then your marriage and spouse, your children next, then your parents, then your extended family and relatives, then fellow believers (your brothers and sisters in Christ), and then the rest of the world.

While sometimes decisions must be made to focus on one person over another, the goal is not to be neglecting any of our life relationships based on God's Word. The biblical balance is allowing God to empower us to meet all of our relationship priorities, inside and outside our families so you can be the person God intends you to be.

One of the most important commitments you can make as a Christian is to read your Bible every day. In each message, we will provide you with a few scriptures to look up and read on your own to plant seeds inside of you for a deeper understanding so you can grow closer to Jesus Christ through His written word.

It's time to get your Bible. For your growing with God, scriptures for the message "What Are Your Priorities in Life Based on Scripture?" are John 14:15, Matthew 22:37–38, and Colossians 3:2.

I pray that this message creates a path for you to grow closer to Jesus Christ or meet Him for the first time. If you want to receive the guaranteed passage that He sacrificed Himself on the cross for so you can be saved as a child of God, then become who you are created to be and turn the words you read in this book into action now so you can have eternal life in the kingdom of heaven that is just waiting for you.

Planting Notes:

_____

_____

_____

_____

_____

Jesus, Can I Get a Do-Over?

I am sure we have all had those moments where we wanted a second or even third chance at something we didn't get right. The interception you threw that lost the big game, that bet you lost and should not have made, your score on a test, and the list can go on and on. We all never want to make mistakes, especially in our life as children of God.

So, can you get a do-over? Have you ever said this to yourself: "Oh, I wish I could have another chance to do that again; I would do it so much better"? Don't fool yourself; we all have said this to ourselves. Why? Because we all want to be better than we are even if we don't know it or know why.

That is proof alone that God is born inside of us. We are gifted as humans to want to be the best people we can, since we were God's creation after all. Why would God ever accept anything less from His children? He only has the best for you when you come to Him.

You should know that feeling of striving for perfection is from God. He always wants you to do things right the first time. That is why He has created a clear path for you to follow through Jesus so you never have to ask yourself that question, so you would never be lost or have regrets as long as you are saved and live by the Word of God.

God will meet you anywhere at any time, even when you're dying as He did the criminals on the cross next to Him. Do you remember the two men who were crucified with Jesus?

They were criminals of the worst sort, deserving death for their crimes. One of them bitterly mocked Jesus and refused to believe in Him, but the other turned to Him in faith and asked Jesus to save him.

He was near death, but Jesus replied, "Truly I tell you, today you will be with me in paradise" (Luke 23:43, NIV). As we can see, this was truly a "deathbed conversion," but God in His grace still saved him after everything he had done to sin against Him.

Don't come to the wrong conclusion about this. Yes, God can save us even at the last minute, but how do we know we'll even have a "last minute"? A sudden accident...an unexpected heart attack... mental disabilities start setting in—hundreds of other things could keep us from turning to Christ and make it too late to get our do-over.

God will meet you anywhere at any time, even when you're dying, but realize that is not an invitation for you to wait until your physical deathbed to call out to Him. As soon as you can comprehend and understand, you are to repent of the sins that you were born into; then, you are to ask to be saved at that moment.

God has created this path for everyone, even infants and those with mental disabilities. God would never leave anyone out, and it is not our job to understand what He can do and how He does it but only to follow His instructions as the child would his father.

God has already prepared a place for you when you come to Him and continually adds to it, as He sees you follow His Word and do as His Son has done for you. Listen: everyone can get on a plane, and they are all on it. But some are in first class and enjoying all the blessings for doing as God instructed them to meet Him in heaven, while others are in the very back seat, squashed in the middle.

Now we are all on the plane (just as we all who are saved will be in heaven) together. But just like with the plane, based on your life according to the Word of God, you could have a first-class seat or be stuck in the very last seat in the middle. No matter what seat you're in, you will still be in heaven.

It is all up to you. Do you want all the blessings of life here and in heaven as a child of God? Or do you want to suffer and anguish as you make your way through a world of sin that only ends in your death and bypassing eternal life?

If you want to get a do-over and be born new again, then just ask Jesus to forgive you of your sins, save you and acknowledge Him as the Lord and Savior of your life. He is always patiently waiting on you. Live by the Word of God in all that you do as you show the way home to others that are lost as you were.

But you must take the first step before it is too late. Yes, there is a point where it is too late to be saved. And that is after your physical death. Without your physical body, you cannot be born again. Just as God used the death of Jesus's physical body to pay the price for your sins at His death: without the death of the physical body of Jesus, He could not have done this.

Can a sinner repent and be saved after death? The answer is no. And there are several passages of Scripture that are clear about that.

"It is appointed for man to die once, and after that comes judgment" (Hebrews 9:27). This scripture expresses that, upon your death, you should expect immediate judgment and not search for any place where you can get a do-over since it does not exist.

So we now know and understand that one of the Bible's greatest truths is that God is willing to forgive us completely, even at the last minute. If you truly commit your life to Christ and trust in Him for your salvation, you can be sure then you will be safe with Jesus forever.

You must come to the conclusion of urgency that you need to do the same thing as Jesus did—by dying on the cross in your former self and leaving your past and everything you were behind you so you can be born new again and get that do-over for your guaranty of eternal life and every blessing that comes with it.

It is important to know it does not matter who you are. God has made His Word so every person can understand it. By doing so, people who resist will have no second chance and an expressway to judgment. I pray to see you in heaven and that judgment does not become your ending.

As a final thought: just think about all the years you have wasted, years you could have lived for Christ and known the joy of His presence. If you've never committed your life to Christ, I urge you to do so today before it's too late.

The Bible says, "Now is the day of salvation" (2 Corinthians 6:2). I believe it is yours; right now, He is calling out for you to come home. Just as a father that loves his child and has a heart of protection over them does because they were his creation and a miracle.

One of the most important commitments you can make as a Christian is to read your Bible every day. In each message, we will provide you with a few scriptures to look up and read on your own to plant seeds inside of you for a deeper understanding so you can grow closer to Jesus Christ through His written word.

It's time to get your Bible. For your growing with God, scriptures for the message "Jesus, Can I Get a Do-Over?" are Luke 9:59–62, 2 Corinthians 5:10, and Acts 16:25–33.

I pray that this message creates a path for you to grow closer to Jesus Christ or meet Him for the first time. If you want to receive the guaranteed passage that He sacrificed Himself on the cross for so you can be saved as a child of God, then become who you are created to be and turn the words you read in this book into action now so you can have eternal life in the kingdom of heaven that is just waiting for you.

Planting Notes:

_____

_____

_____

_____

_____

Seventy-Two Hours

What could possibly be done in only 4,320 minutes or three days and nights that would change the world forever in that short span of time? Throughout time itself, we have seen it take long periods with great thought and planning to perform any changes that affect the world—unless you are Jesus.

So, what if you only had seventy-two hours to change your world forever, if you only had seventy-two hours to live and you knew it. What if you knew you would suffer greatly in the next seventy-two hours in order to do what the Father had sent you for? What would you do?

Would you only think of yourself, or would you do what Jesus did? Do you love God, your brothers and sisters, and all the children of God as much as Jesus did? If you don't and you claim to be a Christian, you need a checkup from the chest up because that is the love God has for you, and you must have it for others.

Let's begin with the seventy-two hours that Jesus lived that changed the world forever so we can understand what love truly is and what was done to save us. The lesson we need to understand is that if you are a Christian and have given yourself to the Lord and Savior to spend eternal life in heaven, there are specific things that will be expected of you.

Will you do the same for others that was done for you on your journey with the King to the gates of heaven? How many will you bring with you? How many have you brought to Jesus that will continue growing His kingdom after you are with God?

We are going to start our journey into the last seventy-two hours of Christ's life, beginning just after midnight in the first hours of Wednesday morning on April 5. Judas is arriving in the Garden of Gethsemane, accompanied by armed officers and other men provided by the religious leaders. For thirty pieces of silver, Judas kissed Him on His cheek, as a signal to identify who Jesus was, so He could be arrested.

So, what we first need to discover is: Would you still love someone that sinned against you by sentencing you to your death as Judas did to Jesus? Is the love of God strong enough that lives in you to forgive even your worst enemy and still protect them like family with your own life?

Jesus is the master of forgiveness, which allows His heart to love everyone regardless of who they are, where they come from, or what sins they have committed against Him. It was an automatic part of His heart as it should be in ours.

Not forgiving creates the hardening of the heart and bitterness of the mind. It literally spoils your soul and rots you from the inside out with sin. Jesus knew what He had to go through in order to complete what God had sent Him for: to save all of us. Would you do the same?

Now we are moving to a couple of hours later. At approximately two a.m., the high priest questions Jesus about His disciples and teachings but does not receive an answer. Frustrated, he demands Him to state whether or not He is the true Son of God. Jesus replies, "But I say to all of you: From now on you will see the Son of Man sitting at the right hand of the Mighty One and coming on the clouds of heaven" (Matthew 26:64, NIV). The answer the high priest receives so angers him that he tears his clothes and cries out that Christ has committed blasphemy. The high priest then immediately asks the council for a verdict, to which they unanimously shout that the death penalty should be carried out.

We are discovering the strength it takes to stand on the truth no matter whether others believe you or not. You know beyond a shadow of a doubt that the truth of the Lord is the only truth that exists, and you will not stray from it at any cost, even death.

It is a fact the truth will set you free. The truth is impenetrable, unbreakable, and undeniable, and it is forever. It saves you from sin and cleanses your soul. It is without question or compromise and convicts or blesses you, based on the path you follow. It breathes life into you and blesses you in everything you do. The one question you must answer is: Will you stand by the truth of God as Jesus did?

At sunrise on Wednesday, just a few short hours after his betrayal, Judas Iscariot returns the thirty pieces of silver and repents of sin he committed on Jesus Christ but still hangs himself.

This is one of the most powerful examples of how fast sin can destroy your life. Once Satan had convinced Judas to betray Jesus, it was the beginning of the end for him. Judas did have a true heart for Jesus, and the sin he committed against Him did so much damage so quickly that Satan convinced Judas to take his own life.

Suicide is a desecration of the temple and is considered self-murder, which is considered to be a sin. But if you are saved, it does not mean you will go to hell and not heaven if you take your own life, as our acceptance into heaven is not based on our obedience but our obedience to Jesus. The Bible views suicide as equal to murder, which is what it is, self-murder. God is the only one who is to decide when and how a person should die: "My times are in your hands" (Psalm 31:15, NIV). Sin is death, and you should never allow it in your life as a child of God in any form.

At roughly eight a.m., Pontius Pilate tells the Jewish religious leaders that he finds Jesus innocent, but he cannot release Him and then has his soldiers severely beat and scourge Jesus. From nine a.m. to noon, Jesus is nailed to the cross. He is crucified along with two thieves.

Near the end of His life, Christ asks God the Father to forgive those that are killing Him. Then, from noon to three p.m., darkness covers the entire land. At three p.m., Jesus Christ, the Savior of man, is forsaken by God and cries out with a loud voice: "My God, my

God, why hast Thou forsaken me" (Matthew 27:46, KJV). In His last moments, Satan tries for a split second with one final attempt to get Jesus to deny God but is unsuccessful. A spear is thrust into His side, and He cries out with a loud voice, "It is finished!" His last words are: "Father, into your hands I commit my spirit" (Luke 23:46, NIV). Jesus is placed in the tomb on Wednesday at sunset.

This is where your faith, belief, and love for God are tested. Could you imagine if you were pronounced innocent and then still be given the punishment of the guilty? Would you still stand firm in your faith as Jesus did? Or would you allow Satan to steal your salvation in the last second?

We are now on Saturday, April 8, in the late afternoon of the weekly Sabbath. Mary Magdalene and the "other Mary" check on where Jesus is buried to anoint Him. Just before sunset, Jesus is *resurrected from the dead* after spending precisely three whole days and three whole nights (seventy-two hours), from sunset on Wednesday to sunset on Saturday, in the tomb!

Hallelujah, hallelujah, hallelujah! Jesus is resurrected and born again. This is absolute proof that the Word of God is the truth and that He is just waiting for us to come to Him and be saved and born again as Jesus was. The resurrection of Jesus was the only way God could, without a doubt, prove His love for you and show you the way home to salvation in the kingdom of heaven as His child.

As a final thought: we have just visited a few of the valuable growth experiences in Christ that all of us should follow as His children. The best way to describe what should be learned in the last seventy-two hours of the life of Jesus Christ is that it is the perfect example of the devotion you should have for your love of the Lord and Savior. You should allow nothing to cause you to deny God, even if it means your own life, to honor the name of the Lord and what He has done for all of us. He is waiting for you with eternal life and love in the kingdom with Him. All you have to do is ask.

One of the most important commitments you can make as a Christian is to read your Bible every day. In each message, we will provide you with a few scriptures to look up and read on your own to plant seeds inside of you for a deeper understanding so you can grow closer to Jesus Christ through His written word.

It's time to get your Bible. For your growing with God, scriptures for the message "Seventy-Two Hours" are John 18:17, 25–27, Acts 1:15–19, and Luke 23:13–15.

I pray that this message creates a path for you to grow closer to Jesus Christ or meet Him for the first time. If you want to receive the guaranteed passage that He sacrificed Himself on the cross for so you can be saved as a child of God, then become who you are created to be and turn the words you read in this book into action now so you can have eternal life in the kingdom of heaven that is just waiting for you.

Planting Notes:

_____

_____

_____

_____

_____

Your Today Does Not Have to Be like Your Yesterday or Tomorrow

Throughout life, I have heard people say, "Oh, I am glad today is over" or "I am glad today is behind me, and I hope I never have another day like that again." The only question is: If you really want your best day every day, what are you doing to make sure that happens?

What does "today does not have to be like yesterday or tomorrow" mean? Are you saved? Are you walking with the Lord every day? Are you following the ways of the world? Do you think you have forever to be saved and it can never be too late?

If you continue to wait to be saved, your yesterday will be like your tomorrow because nothing will have changed, and you are on course to bypass eternal life and choose death. But if you ask Jesus to come into your life today, then your tomorrow will be brand-new every day, and you will never see the yesterdays or tomorrows that you have right now in your life.

Jesus did not say, "Oh, sorry, I missed you yesterday." For one, Jesus never misses anyone: if someone comes to be saved, He is there 24/7/365 for eternity waiting on him or her. Jesus never said, "I will, just see you tomorrow." Jesus said, "Right here, right now, no matter who you are or what you have done, you can be forgiven by asking repentance for your sins and accepting Me as your Lord and Savior."

So how does your today not become like your yesterday and your current tomorrow? You repent of your sins and ask forgiveness from Jesus Christ and for Him to come into your life to be saved right now, today. This is the only way you can make your today different from your yesterday or your tomorrow. You leave your old self behind the second you are saved and become new and born again in Christ.

Your tomorrow will be new as a child of God forevermore, and you will never see another yesterday, as the former you no longer exists.

After you have accepted the Lord and Savior, you need to find a church that preaches from the Bible to be baptized.

So how do you get to know Jesus? This simple yet life-changing question is the most important question that can be asked. *How can I be saved?* deals with where we will spend eternity after our lives in this world are over. There is no more important issue than our eternal destiny. Thankfully, the Bible is abundantly clear in Acts 16:30–31 on how a person can be saved: "'Sirs, what must I do to be saved?' [...] 'Believe in the Lord Jesus, and you will be saved.'"

How can I be saved? Why do I need to be saved? We are all born with sin in us. We are born with sin, and we all personally choose to sin. Sin is what makes us unsaved. Sin is what separates us from God. Sin is what has us on the path to eternal destruction and bypassing eternal life in heaven, choosing death instead.

What am I being saved from? Your sin: we all deserve death. While the physical consequence of sin is physical death, that is not the only kind of death that results from sin. All sin is ultimately committed against God that, once committed, cannot change, only be washed away. Because of that, the just penalty for our sin is also eternal. What we need to be saved from is eternal destruction and ultimately bypassing death. You can only do that by being saved through Jesus Christ.

How can I be saved? How can God provide salvation? The penalty for sin is eternal; only God could pay the penalty because only He is eternal without end.

But because of God's divine nature, He could not die. So He came to us as a human being in the person of Jesus Christ. God took on human flesh, lived among us, and taught us the way, the truth, and the life He had waiting for all of us who believed in Him.

When people turned against Him and His message and wanted to kill Him, He, without hesitation, sacrificed Himself for us, allowing Himself to be crucified and tortured because of His love for us. Because Jesus Christ was human, He could die, and because Jesus Christ was God, His death brought eternal salvation to the human race. Jesus's death on the cross was perfect and the complete payment for our sins forever. He took the punishment we deserved. Jesus's resurrection from death proved His death was a perfectly sufficient sacrifice for the payment of our sin.

How can I be saved? What do I need to do? Believe in Jesus Christ, and you will be saved: God has already done all of the work. All you must do is receive, in faith, the salvation God offers and accept Him as your Lord and Savior. Trust in Jesus alone as the payment for your sins. Believe in Him, and you will not perish as God is offering you salvation as a gift, so it is free for the asking. All you have to do is accept it. Jesus Christ is the only way to salvation.

As it says in Scripture, sin breaks our close relationship with God. It causes us to fear God and try to live our lives outside of His will. We have all heard that the wages of sin is death (Romans 6:23), *but* the gift of God is eternal life through Jesus Christ, our Lord, and is just waiting for you. Come right now to become who God intended you to be with eternal life in the kingdom of heaven.

Remember: God has already done everything for you to restore your relationship with Him. He took the initiative. Now He waits for each of us individually to accept what He has done for us and become saved as the children of God who we are intended to be.

One of the most important commitments you can make as a Christian is to read your Bible every day. In each message, we will provide you with a few scriptures to look up and read on your own to plant seeds inside of you for a deeper understanding so you can grow closer to Jesus Christ through His written word.

It's time to get your Bible. For your growing with God, scriptures for the message "Your Today Does Not Have to Be like Your Yesterday or Tomorrow" are Matthew 25:46, Revelation 20:15, John 10:15.

I pray that this message creates a path for you to grow closer to Jesus Christ or meet Him for the first time. If you want to receive the guaranteed passage that He sacrificed Himself on the cross for so you can be saved as a child of God, then become who you are created to be and turn the words you read in this book into action now so you can have eternal life in the kingdom of heaven that is just waiting for you.

Planting Notes:

_____

_____

_____

_____

_____

His Final Commandment
before Crucifixion

If you were innocent and wrongly being put to death and had one final statement you could make before your death that would bless all of humanity if it was followed, what would that statement be? Would you even care about those left behind and only focus on your own circumstance?

What was the last commandment Jesus gave before His arrest, mock trial, and crucifixion? Do you know? Should you know? Is your life as a child of God affected by it? Does it affect being saved?

So to understand the Word of God better, we first must acknowledge that all of the commandments from God had been given in the Old Testament, but Jesus gave us a new commandment. As a matter of fact, it was the last commandment that Jesus gave before He was arrested, had a mock trial, and then was crucified on the cross.

So what was the last commandment Jesus said before the end of the beginning took place? His last commandment to all of us was we are to love one another as God commands. This is the light of God shining as bright as when you love one another as God loves you. Why is that? Because God sacrificed His Son for you because He loves you so much.

What is loving one another? Why are we supposed to love one another? What does God say about loving one another? What happens if I do not follow His commandment and love one another equally? These are many questions we need to be answered to be all God has intended us to be and to follow His Word as His children.

Let's look at the scripture of John 13:34 for a deeper understanding of His word: "A new commandment I give to you, that you love one another: just as I have loved you, you also are to love one another."

The Bible clearly states that He commands us to love one another. He does not give you an option or say, "Go ahead and think about it." Although there is a choice to follow His word that you are given to love as He expects from you, that love should be your heart's desire to love one another, as it is His heart's desire to love us for eternity. If love was something we would do on our own as His children, then He would have had no need to make it His final commandment before His crucifixion.

Let's see what God says about how we are supposed to love in the scripture of 1 John 4:20: "If anyone says, 'I love God,' and hates his brother, he is a liar; for he who does not love his brother whom he has seen cannot love God whom he has not seen."

As you can clearly see, God will not acknowledge your love for Him if you do not love your brother as God has proven to love you. But it is not just the love you had received, knowing Jesus, but a new spirit-filled, holy love; it is a giving love that God expects you not to wrong your neighbor or brother only but to lift them up to God. Place them ahead of your own needs in the name of the Lord, even if they may not deserve it, as we don't deserve His love; we deserve death without Him, as we are sinners without the love of God as our Savior.

There is a purpose as to why God commands that we love one another as it shows in the scripture of John 13:35: "By this all people will know that you are My disciples: if you have love for one another."

God knows your heart better than you do, so this is a clear sign to Him you are His child and are following His Word and commandments.

Now we are going to look at the scripture of Romans 5:8 (NIV): "But God demonstrates his own love for us in this: While we were still sinners Christ died for us." This is an example of how God loves us even though we are not worthy and full of sin, meaning everyone can come to Him.

The most important lesson we must learn about His final commandment before the crucifixion is to love one another through obedience as His Word instructs us. God's Word is for you to know that love is not giving someone what they deserve but what they need as God did you.

There is no better way to glorify God than loving one another no matter who they are or what they have done, whether you know them or they are lost, waiting for you to bring them home to Jesus, as He expects from you as His child to do.

One of the most important commitments you can make as a Christian is to read your Bible every day. In each message, we will provide you with a few scriptures to look up and read on your own to plant seeds inside of you for a deeper understanding so you can grow closer to Jesus Christ through His written word.

It's time to get your Bible. For your growing with God, scriptures for the message "His Final Commandment before Crucifixion" are 1 Corinthians 16:14, 1 Peter 4:8, and Ephesians 5:21.

I pray that this message creates a path for you to grow closer to Jesus Christ or meet Him for the first time. If you want to receive the guaranteed passage that He sacrificed Himself on the cross for so you can be saved as a child of God, then become who you are created to be and turn the words you read in this book into action now so you can have eternal life in the kingdom of heaven that is just waiting for you.

Planting Notes:

_____

_____

_____

_____

Jesus Is Coming: Does He Know You?

Most people, when they knock on a door to go into a home of people they do not know, will usually get a chilly response like, "Who are you? I don't know you; you are a stranger." That is because there is no existence of a relationship between them. As Christians, we know the most important thing is to have a relationship with Jesus Christ in order to enter into heaven.

Let's start our message with a question: When Jesus comes back, will He know you? Let's not get confused; I am not asking you if you know Him. I am asking you if He knows you. Could you imagine how terrifying it would be if the second coming was here and you were standing right in front of Jesus, yelling at Him, and He did not hear or see you?

Could that really happen? Why would that happen? Let's take a look at what happens the very second we become deceased. There are actually several reasons you could cause this to happen in your life.

First, immediately upon death, each person undergoes their particular judgment and, depending upon one's behavior on the earth and whether they were saved or not, goes to heaven or hell. Those in hell will never reach heaven and will be in hell for eternity.

Well, we all know what heaven and hell are, so we now know that one of the two things will happen when we die, based on if Jesus does not know us when He returns during the second coming or when we become deceased. So we have learned that you not only must know Jesus, but He must know you as well.

You know exactly where you will go and what to expect if you do not know Jesus and He does not know you. So, another key to salvation has unlocked more wisdom. Therefore, let's see what the Scriptures say about the fact that Jesus is supposed to know you and not just that you are supposed to know Him.

First, let's begin with John 14:6: "Jesus said to him, 'I am the way, and the truth, and the life. No one comes to the Father except through me.'"

So, we know that means no one can come to the Father except through Jesus. So, in order for that to take place, Jesus would have to recognize you and know who you are. I guess the question is, does He?

Our next scripture is Jeremiah 17:10: "I the LORD search the heart and test the mind, to give every man according to his ways, according to the fruit of his deeds." In this scripture, it is very clear that Jesus is searching you to see if He knows you and what Jesus does see, He will act on, according to the way you have lived your life as the Father's child and according to His Word.

Our closing scripture for this part of the message telling us that Jesus must know you and who you are is Psalm 139:23–24: "Search me, O God, and know my heart! Try me and know my thoughts! And see if there be any grievous way in me, and lead me in the way everlasting!"

In this scripture, you are pleading with Jesus to know you because you are now fully aware of what will happen if He does not know you at death. You are asking Jesus to search through all of you—heart, mind, and soul—and find anything that is bad and unholy. Then you are asking Jesus to do whatever it takes to remove it from you so He can see you and know you in eternal life with Him.

Well, we should all have a clear understanding that not only must we know Jesus, but He must know us as well. So, that leads us to the next question: What do you do to guarantee that Jesus will know you?

Because the last thing you want to happen is to hear what Philip did in John 14:9 when Jesus said to him, "Have I been with you so long, and you still do not know me, Philip? Whoever has seen me has seen the Father. How can you say, 'Show us the Father'?"

Now, let's discover how you can guarantee Jesus will know you.

The first step so that Jesus will know you is for you to recognize that, according to the Bible, you are a sinner and have fallen short of God's standard He expects from His children. You have broken God's laws (the Ten Commandments). You must understand that you are a natural-born sinner and deserve God's correction for choosing selfishness over Him.

Next, you must come to the biblical understanding that Christ died for you and that His death on the cross was His paying the penalty for your and my sins. He willingly took the punishment for your sins while you were like a stranger and like an "enemy" to Him.

Now, according to Christianity, consistent with the Bible, you must repent and turn away from your sins once and for all. Ask Jesus to forgive you of your sins and surrender your life to Him. Confess with your mouth that Jesus Christ is the Lord and believe in your heart that God raised Him from the dead and you will be saved.

"All things work together for good to those who love God, to those who are called according to His purpose" (Romans 8:28, NKJV). You can start to gain ground as a brother or sister of Jesus by confessing with your mouth that Jesus is the Lord and agreeing with Jesus's means: to be born again of water and the Spirit to enter into the kingdom of God.

Get your own Bible and start reading it and praying daily immediately, and you will come to realize the phrase "God is like the air you breathe." If you do not know how to breathe, then how can you really be alive and a child of God, and how can Jesus know who you are?

Find a church that teaches and preaches directly from the Bible and believes in salvation through repentance and faith in Jesus alone as is opposed to any alternative tradition not based on the principles and the words of the Bible and the Father, the Son, and the Holy Spirit.

Talk to a pastor, or any other kind of Christian, such as a spiritual leader—and tell him about the decision you have just made to repent of your sins and proclaim Jesus Christ as your Lord and Savior and get baptized to publicly proclaim the spiritual transformation and faith you now have and that you are born again new as a child of God.

You must open all of yourself up with not one part of you held back in repentance in order to receive Jesus Christ by confessing your sins to God, praying, and asking to receive the Holy Spirit and forgiveness to be who God intended you to be.

Finally, avoid sabotaging your prayer life, so be sure to pray effectually and efficiently. "And when you pray, do not use vain repetitions as the heathen do. For they think that they shall be heard for their many words" (Matthew 6:7, NKJV). Do as Matthew 6:7 instructs and believe and accept that God already knows, cares, and is always there for you as His child He will see in the kingdom of heaven.

One of the most important commitments you can make as a Christian is to read your Bible every day. In each message, we will provide you with a few scriptures to look up and read on your own to plant seeds inside of you for a deeper understanding so you can grow closer to Jesus Christ through His written word.

It's time to get your Bible. For your growing with God, scriptures for the message "Jesus Is Coming: Does He Know You?" are Matthew 7:21–23, John 13:35, and Revelation 1:7.

I pray that this message creates a path for you to grow closer to Jesus Christ or meet Him for the first time. If you want to receive the guaranteed passage that He sacrificed Himself on the cross for so you can be saved as a child of God, then become who you are created to be and turn the words you read in this book into action now so you can have eternal life in the kingdom of heaven that is just waiting for you.

Planting Notes:

_____

_____

_____

_____

_____

Jesus Is Coming:
the Signs Are Here

We spend our lives looking for signs to process what our reactions will be to different information: thunder and clouds for a rainstorm coming, stop or yield signs, "danger ahead," railroad tracks, merge, a smile, exit and enter, and the list goes on. But so many do not know what the signs are when Jesus returns.

Jesus is coming again. Scripture declares what God has done and will do in John 14:2–3 (NKJV):

> In My Father's house are many mansions; if it were not so, I would have told you. I go to prepare a place for you. And if I go and prepare a place for you, I will come again and receive you to Myself; that where I am, there you may be also.

This is undeniable proof that Jesus will return for His people. He is so sure that He has already prepared a place for you in His kingdom upon His return. The Bible is truth and only speaks the truth, so it is written; therefore, it shall be and will come to pass.

In part one of this chapter, we are going to look at what are the signs for the second coming and explore Scripture that validates those points are fact and truth. Then, in the coming messages, we will break down each sign for the return of Jesus so that you have the exact understanding to know when God is coming and what to look for so you are aware of the Lord's arrival.

Can the unimaginable really happen in your lifetime? Do you know what the most important worldwide event of our generation will be that will shake the world to its knees immediately? The second coming of Christ will be the most important event of this generation. Christ is coming back! Hallelujah, hallelujah, hallelujah!

This is an absolute. Jesus will return, and it will not happen secretly, off in some cave, with no one knowing about it. Jesus Christ will literally come back to the city of Jerusalem, to the top of the Mount of Olives, to begin governing the entire earth! There will be a divine, one-world government. What a shock that will be to all of humanity!

If the King of kings is soon returning to establish the kingdom of God upon this earth, you should be getting ready for it. You should know how it will affect every area of who you are as His child or a nonbeliever.

Are we living in the last days? Non-Christians will find it hard to believe we are living in the last days of earth's history.

> First, I want to remind you that in the last days there will come scoffers who will do every wrong they can think of and laugh at the truth. This will be their line of argument: "So Jesus promised to come back, did He? Then where is He? He'll never come! Why, as far back as anyone can remember, everything has remained exactly as it was since the first day of creation."

> 2 Peter 3:3–4 (TLB)

Let's get started with a scripture that tells us that there will be the second coming of Christ, Matthew 24:3,

> As Jesus was sitting on the Mount of Olives, the disciples came to him privately. "Tell us," they said, "when will this happen? and what will be the sign of your coming and of the end of the age?"

His own disciples were asking Jesus, "When will You return, and how will we know? How will we recognize what the signs to look for are so we know when to expect Your arrival?"

The gospels of Matthew, Mark, and Luke each contain an account of Christ teaching His disciples what to watch for before He returns. Luke wrote,

> So you also, when you see these things happening, know that the kingdom of God is near. Assuredly, I say to you, this generation will by no means pass away till all things take place. Heaven and earth will pass away, but My words will by no means pass away.

> Luke 21:31–33 (NKJV)

What are the signs of the second coming of Christ? One of the very clear signs to see that the return of Christ is coming near will be wars, violence, and lawlessness; though they may seem overwhelming and appear as if the end is coming, it will not be the end. Matthew 24:6 (NIV) says, "You will hear of wars and rumors of wars, but see to it that you are not alarmed. Such things must happen, but the end is still to come."

There is no denying this sign is alive and ticking the clock down to the return of Jesus. Look at the turmoil and lawlessness our nation and world have suffered in just recent history.

The next sign of the second coming is earthquakes, droughts, famine, and other natural catastrophes. "There will be famines and earthquakes in various places. All these are the beginning of birth pains" (Matthew 24:7–8, NIV).

Look at the global natural disasters and devastation in our country with fires and tornados.

Disease epidemics: to ensure His power was understood, God has used plagues and diseases on both believers and those who opposed Him several times throughout the Bible. The power that He could protect His followers from the hardship that the enemy was suffering was so undeniable it displayed His ultimate control over all illnesses.

You would literally have to be wearing a blindfold and earplugs in order to not know about the global disease pandemic that is occurring right now with no end in sight as one new strain after another seems to emerge with no explanation. That has, in about one year, taken 560,000 plus lives just in the United States.

A great false religious leader will appear who will be the Antichrist and is another sign of the end approaching. First John 2:18 (NKJV) says, "Little children, it is the last hour; and as you have heard that the Antichrist is coming, even now many antichrists have come, by which we know that it is the last hour."

Unholy imposters posing as Jesus will try to deceive people in the last days.

> At that time if anyone says to you, "Look, here is the Messiah!" or, "There he is!" do not believe it. For false messiahs and false prophets will appear and perform great signs and wonders to deceive, if possible, even the elect.
>
> Matthew 24:23–24 (NIV)

The *collapse of morality and humanity* will be the moral breakdown of the character of society in the last days:

> But mark this: There will be terrible times in the last days. People will be lovers of themselves, lovers of money, boastful, proud, abusive, disobedient to their parents, ungrateful, unholy, without love, unforgiving, slander-ous, without self-control, brutal, not lovers of the good, treacherous, rash, conceited, lovers of pleasure rather than lovers of God—having a form of godliness but denying its power. Have nothing to do with them.
>
> 2 Timothy 3:1–5 (NIV)

Does this sound like anyone you know? Have you seen people behave in this manner? Are you experiencing this in your own life? Do you have any type of relationship with these types of people? Are you one of these types of people? These are people who act as if they are holy and godly but deny that God is the reason for all that is in life and that He exists. God will have nothing to do with these types of sinners.

We have covered just a few of the signs for the second coming of Jesus Christ. We will explore more, based on Scripture, in the next chapter and break each one down.

Now, let's review all of the signs of the second coming of Jesus that you need to know and be aware of in order to be prepared to go home with the Father and the Son in the kingdom of heaven.

Signs of the second coming that accelerate the return of Jesus:

➤ Wars, violence, and lawlessness
➤ Droughts and famine
➤ Earthquakes and other natural catastrophes
➤ Disease epidemics
➤ The rise of an aggressive fundamentalist Islamic power
➤ An ascendant European union seeking global primacy
➤ A powerful religious figure leading a religious revival
➤ A great false religious leader appearing
➤ The gospel of the kingdom of God preached to all nations
➤ Faith again becoming a matter of life or death
➤ A crisis striking Jerusalem
➤ The abomination of desolation
➤ The great tribulation—the collapse of the English-speaking nations
➤ The pivotal Old Testament prophecy
➤ God's promises to deliver His people
➤ Heavenly signs and the day of the Lord
➤ The seven last plagues

What lies ahead? What should you do?

One of the most important commitments you can make as a Christian is to read your Bible every day. In each message, we will provide you with a few scriptures to look up and read on your own to plant seeds inside of you for a deeper understanding so you can grow closer to Jesus Christ through His written word.

It's time to get your Bible. For your growing with God, scriptures for the message "Jesus Is Coming: the Signs are Here" are Matthew 24:14, Matthew 24:27, and Revelation 22:12.

I pray that this message creates a path for you to grow closer to Jesus Christ or meet Him for the first time. If you want to receive the guaranteed passage that He sacrificed Himself on the cross for so you can be saved as a child of God, then become who you are created to be and turn the words you read in this book into action now so you can have eternal life in the kingdom of heaven that is just waiting for you.

Planting Notes:

_____

_____

_____

_____

_____

THE FOUR HORSEMEN

It would be hard to comprehend or even imagine the ultimate ungodly punishment of death and suffering among all those who deserve, unleashing all over the earth, according to the end of days in Revelations. The sole purpose of the four horsemen of the Apocalypse is to reign the final judgment over the world.

In this message, we are going to explore the four horsemen of Revelation to have a deeper understanding of God's Word. Who are the four horsemen? What do the four horsemen do? Why do you need to know about them?

The last book of the New Testament, named Revelations, is where we are introduced to Satan's army called the four horsemen and the first four of the seven seals of God. The first four seals of the seven seals are punishments from God, known as pestilence, war, famine, and death that will occur during the Apocalypse.

Here is where it all begins: the four horsemen appear when the Lamb of God opens the first four seals on the scroll He receives from God. These four horsemen represent threats that would have been real for people in the New Testament times and people of future time, meaning today.

These four horsemen are designed to make people aware of their own weaknesses and vulnerability. As these and other threats appear in relentless succession, people are moved to ask, "Who can stand?"

> I watched as the Lamb opened the first of the seven seals
> [...] I looked, and there before me was a white horse! Its

rider held a bow, and he was given a crown, and he rode out as a conqueror bent on conquest.

Revelation 6:1–2 (NIV)

The first seal opens at the beginning of the final seven-year tribulation leading up to the second coming.

The first seal is opened, revealing the coming Antichrist riding a white horse. No one will be able to turn away from the ultimate power this person displays even though he is Satan's version of Christ (a false god). Then the second seal is opened, revealing the red horse bringing war and bloodshed throughout the world. God's first judgment for rejecting Christ in this world will bring peace in the first half of seven years and war in the last half of seven years after the first seal is opened.

> When he opened the second seal, I heard the second living creature call out, "Come!" And out came another horse, bright red; its rider was permitted to remove peace from the earth, so that people would slaughter one another; and he was given a great sword.

Revelation 6:3–4

Red equals blood, and blood equals war.

This rider takes peace from the earth. This seal is opened in the middle of the tribulation when the Abomination of Desolation is set up in the Temple in Jerusalem. Jesus discussed this in Matthew, chapter twenty-four. Let's remember what war really is:

> When the Lamb opened the third seal, I heard the third living creature call out, "Come!" I looked, and there was a black horse! Its rider held a pair of scales in his hand.

Revelation 6:5 (NIV)

As you learn about the third seal that is opened, you would almost believe it has already been opened, along with seal one, based on what we have been experiencing as a world in the last twenty-four months, with the pandemic and the prices of everything skyrocketing and with supplies getting more and more unavailable, adding decades of global wars to our history. There are many who may say the Apocalypse has already begun, meaning the Antichrist could be in the world today but has not revealed himself yet.

The third seal is opened, and the black horse appears, spreading famine across the world. Food shortages combined with explosive price increases eliminate access to food for millions all around the world. It becomes a time of those who have and have not, devastating the wealthiest of nations in the world within two years and all other countries within one year if crop failures occur worldwide, creating global starvation.

> When he opened the fourth seal, I heard the voice of the fourth living creature call out, "Come!" I looked and there was a pale green horse! Its rider's name was Death, and Hades followed with him; they were given authority over a fourth of the earth, to kill with sword and with famine and with pestilence and by wild beasts of the earth.
>
> Revelation 6:7–8

What is the result of war and famine? Death.

There is a science fiction movie once where the world is running out of food. The elites are given green blocks of food to eat and survive. Then it is discovered that the green blocks are human remains dressed up for consumption. This is the pale horse.

"One-fourth of the people on earth die." Currently, that's about two billion people. This is an incredible amount of death. It's estimated that only one hundred million have died in all of the wars on the earth to date!

We all have seen how war devastates nations forever, leaving a trail of death and famine behind its path of destruction. But this is only the beginning, as the fourth seal is opened, bringing death to 25% of the world or around 2 billion people. There have only been about 100 million people dying in all wars throughout history—to understand a comparison of devastation. Even movies have depicted horrific images of human remains during these times, being used as a disguised food source for survivors due to the combination of all of these events subjecting the world to the wrath of God for disobedience.

Who could even imagine these types of events being reality one day in the future and one-fourth of the world falling to death, but they will be coming. For certain, if the world can be created by God, it also can definitely be destroyed by Him as well. We actually get to see what the future has, giving us one final chance to turn to Christ as our Savior before it is too late. God lets us experience an example of what we can expect, whether our ultimate destination is hell or heaven.

Good news! Did you know that the book of Revelation says that those who read and study Revelation will receive a special blessing? So, let's be blessed and open the book and read every word.

Our last scripture in this message will be Psalm 130:1 (NIV): "If you, O LORD, kept a record of sins, O Lord, who could stand? But with you there is forgiveness; therefore you are feared." Those who belong to God and the Lamb are able to stand in the face of these threats.

How important is it that you are saved as a child of God? That you repent from your sin and ask for forgiveness from Jesus Christ? How incredible that God has given you a way to bypass the seven seals of the four horsemen's wrath as He returns to reclaim His creation!

One of the most important commitments you can make as a Christian is to read your Bible every day. In each message, we will provide you with a few scriptures to look up and read on your own to plant seeds inside of you for a deeper understanding so you can grow closer to Jesus Christ through His written word.

It's time to get your Bible. For your growing with God, scriptures for the message "The Four Horsemen" are Revelation 6:1–8, Revelation 7:1–17, and Revelation 5:1–14.

I pray that this message creates a path for you to grow closer to Jesus Christ or meet Him for the first time. If you want to receive the guaranteed passage that He sacrificed Himself on the cross for so you can be saved as a child of God, then become who you are created to be and turn the words you read in this book into action now so you can have eternal life in the kingdom of heaven that is just waiting for you.

Planting Notes:

_____

_____

_____

_____

_____

The Power of Compounding Christ (Thirty-Day Discipleship Devotion)

Most people are interested in knowing how they can grow their wealth as fast as possible. How do they become rich beyond belief? Is there some magic formula they need to know about in order to do that? Is this knowledge available to every person on the earth? Yes, it is available for everyone if you're looking for it in the right place. Honestly, this revealed secret is just waiting for you to find it to provide you with more than you could ever desire or imagine.

Have you ever heard the saying "If you double one penny every day, then at the end of thirty days, you will have a million dollars"? Actually, over $5 million…which is true. What if you used that same proven method to ask the lost if they died today if they believed they would go to heaven? What if you asked one person a day and had the person you asked do the same thing every day?

Oh, wait a minute…isn't that what we are supposed to do anyway as followers of Jesus Christ, to do exactly what He does, as we are made in His image? Just like a penny, we all look the same, yet everyone is just a little different from the other. But yet, if you add them all together, they create great wealth. Just like there is no greater wealth than to be saved and have eternal life in the kingdom of heaven with all of your brothers and sisters.

Simple enough: if you instruct every person you ask to do the same as you are doing, do you realize you could bring over one million people to know who Jesus Christ is in just thirty days by following this method of saving the lost?

What if there were thousands of people doing this all over the world? What if you had everyone you know or your church start this immediately? How much could we glorify God in just the next thirty days?

We turn to Him for comfort in our sufferings, and He turns to us to help. Jesus endured His passion so that He could save the souls of sinners. Jesus communicated to the world that He can use our sufferings to save souls if we join them in His passion. The greatest need of Jesus is to rescue the suffering souls of the Father's children.

Now, let's just cover a few scriptures on saving souls. First, we will start with Proverbs 11:30 (KJV): "The fruit of the righteous is a tree of life; and he that winneth souls is wise."

God is speaking about the souls you bring Him to save through His Son, Jesus Christ, how they will be branches of your blessed, filled life, as He knows that you have done the most important things there are for God, bringing His children to Jesus so they can be saved and come home to Him. You have become like Jesus. How pleased God is with you as His child.

> My brothers and sisters, if one of you should wander
> from the truth and someone should bring that person
> back, remember this: Whoever turns a sinner from the
> error of their way will save them from death and cover
> over a multitude of sins.

> James 5:19–20 (NIV)

Jesus is telling you that if any of the Father's children are lost or become lost in their walk with Him and that if you are responsible for bringing His child to Jesus, then they will be forgiven and saved by your actions so that they are washed of sin and born new again.

I would like to offer a challenge to you and everyone you know and even those you have not met or are about to meet. If you accept this commitment to our Lord and Savior, then you will take up the cross, step out in your faith, and become the disciple for God that is inside of every one of His children. I guess the questions are:

Will you be the penny and carry the cross?

Will you challenge yourself to do this as His disciple?

Will you challenge everyone you know to do this?

Will you challenge your church to do this?

Do you love Jesus as much as He loves you?

How many of your lost brothers and sisters can be saved in the next thirty days? Hundreds or even millions…

One of the most important commitments you can make as a Christian is to read your Bible every day. In each message, we will provide you with a few scriptures to look up and read on your own to plant seeds inside of you for a deeper understanding so you can grow closer to Jesus Christ through His written word.

It's time to get your Bible. For your growing with God, scriptures for the message "The Power of Compounding Christ (Thirty-Day Discipleship Devotion)" are Matthew 28:18–20, Matthew 5:14–16, and Ephesians 4:11–17.

I pray that this message creates a path for you to grow closer to Jesus Christ or meet Him for the first time. If you want to receive the guaranteed passage that He sacrificed Himself on the cross for so you can be saved as a child of God, then become who you are created to be and turn the words you read in this book into action now so you can have eternal life in the kingdom of heaven that is just waiting for you.

Planting Notes:

_____

_____

_____

_____

_____

How to Have Your Best Relationship with God Now

We all, for some reason, desire the best things in life that we can have. The best job, car, home, wife, family, life, and heaven if you are a Christian. In our world of imperfection, we are always in the pursuit of perfection. But many of us are not putting that same ambition into our spiritual life and walk with God, leaving the question: How do you go about having your best life with God now?

The first thing you need to understand is that your best life now with God is 100 percent based on your personal relationship with Him. The first thing we are going to make very clear is how *not to have* your best life with God now.

If you decide to act in the following ways, you will never have the relationship with God He wants from you as His child. If you are a person who is full of sin, unresolved issues as a child or adult, you can't or won't lay down to God, with unforgiving spirit and the fear of transparency, then these are blocking your way and bypassing eternal life and leading you to death in this world.

Now that we have clearly understood what we are not supposed to do to have our best relationship with God, we will now focus on what you must do to have your best relationship with God now. By following these simple guidelines, you will always stay exactly where God wants you to be to have the amazing relationship that a loving father and child have together.

The first thing we are going to discuss is time. Time is the most valuable thing that you own in life that is not replaceable. Once it is gone, it is gone forever. So that means you only have a certain amount of time to be saved and have a relationship with the Father and the Son to guarantee eternal life in heaven. Yes, you do not have forever to be saved, as there will be a time when it is too late and you have become part of the world that exists no more.

We are not talking about attending church or fellowshipping with other believers; we are talking about the one-on-one time where there is no noise, no distractions, where you are in that special place that is just for you and God. If you don't have one, then please find that place in your life. That is where you build your most intimate relationship with God.

None of us wants anyone around us when we are being intimate with others and having those moments where we become close to one another in a very personal way. That is where you meet God to have your best life with Him now. With that same intimacy, love, care, and giving of yourself to one another with your mind, body, and soul. This is the time God wants with you the most, and He will give you your best life with Him now when you share it with Him.

We will now explore our first scripture in this message with Matthew 6:6: "But when you pray, go into your room and shut the door and pray to your Father who is in secret. And your Father who sees in secret will reward you."

The next thing we must do to have our best relationship with God now is to listen intently and focus. If you do not listen, then how are you supposed to be able to hear anything? The great thing about God is your time with Him is just between you and Him, and He requires that of you. So if you are allowing anything to enter the space that is just for you and God, He may not hear you. Keep your mind clear of the world so He can hear you and you can hear Him.

The next scripture we will explore in this message is John 8:47: "Whoever is of God hears the words of God. The reason why you do not hear, is that you are not of God." As you can see in this verse, God clearly wants that quiet personal space where you are together and you listen to Him and He listens to you.

If that space and time does not exist so you can hear one another, then how will you ever even have a relationship with Him? There is a saying that has been around for a long time, "you have two ears and one mouth for a reason." You are supposed to listen twice as much as you speak. This applies directly to putting others in front of your own desires. If you are speaking twice as much as you listen, then you never hear anything that is ever said to you by anyone except yourself.

As we continue to learn what is necessary for our best relationship with God now, we must be totally 100 percent transparent. See through, as there can be nothing you are hiding inside of you or blocking your relationship with God. God will see it anyway, so why hide it and fool yourself when you can just give it to God and let Him take care of it for you?

Things can only be clear when they are perfectly transparent; otherwise, they are blurry and confusing, intended for you to lose your way. You can't see anyone through anything that appears unclear. To be transparent means to be present with God in the same space, and nothing else matters but for you to hear Him and for Him to hear you.

The next thing you must do with God to have your best relationship now is to display your true feelings to Him in your relationship. God only knows and only speaks words of truth, and He shares His feeling with you in His love story called the Bible. So you know exactly what to expect from Him in any situation at any time.

Because God loves you so much and never wants you to forget His true feelings for you, He sent His only Son to be sacrificed on the cross and bring the truth of His Word to the world so you can be saved and have eternal life with Him in the kingdom of heaven. Nothing greater could be done, so you know God's true feelings for you.

You must never show anything less than what you truly feel to God. Imagine if you went to the doctor to get cured and you did not tell him the real truth. How could you ever expect to be saved from what is making you sick? The absolute truth that you share with God is how you can have your best relationship with Him now.

One of the main ways we build the best relationship with God is through emotionally honest prayers where we are expressing our feelings to Him.

Our next step in understanding how we can have the best relationship with God now is you must have the blessing of forgiveness in your heart and spirit. If you are unable to do this, you will never do as Jesus did with forgiveness all the way to the cross. Forgiveness is another form of loving someone in a manner that is holy to God and expected by Him from you.

Forgiveness mends the heart to be stronger than it was before because it is an act of holiness by you toward others. If you are unable to forgive anyone or anything through Christ, then you will be sinning against God's Word. Forgiveness is a cornerstone of Christianity, and Jesus, in His last breath, said, "Father, forgive them, for they do not know what they do" (Luke 23:34, NKJV).

Now, let's explore the scripture of Ephesians 4:32: "Be kind to one another, tenderhearted, forgiving one another, as God in Christ forgave you." This clearly points out God's commandment of forgiveness is to be a part of you as His child.

If you have never forgiven someone, how do you know you truly love them? Forgiveness brings you closer to Jesus Christ. Every time you offer that blessing to someone, you actually benefit more than they do, as it pleases God that you follow His Word in all ways.

Now, we will explore the final four elements of having your best relationship with God with trust, understanding, love, and approval so you can be all God intends you to be by having the best relationship you can with Him now and forever.

Up to this point, we have shared five ways to have your best relationship with God now, and they were: spending one-on-one time with God, intently listening, as we are supposed to listen twice as much as we speak; we have to be 100 percent transparent with God, as there can be nothing between Him and us in order for Him to know we are there; we must always show our true and honest feelings to God no matter what they are, and we must have the same heart of forgiveness as Jesus does.

We will now explore the remaining four elements necessary for you to have your best relationship with God now. The first element we are exploring in part two is *trust*. Without trust, there is nothing and absolutely no way for a holy relationship with you and God or you and anyone else to even exist.

Trust is the glue of your words; it is the action of your life; it is the character of who you are; it is the belief in yourself and others in you; it is the cornerstone of faith that you know God is always there for you; it is the core of relationships with others; it is the foundation of love, and it is necessary for your best relationship with God now.

In our first scripture in part two, we are going to explore Proverbs 3:5–6: "Trust in the Lord with all your heart, and do not lean on your own understanding. In all your ways acknowledge him, and he will make straight your paths." As we can see, God wants our trust in Him to be the core of who we are and wants you to know there is nothing else you are to trust in, as He will always light the path on your way.

We will continue with the next element we need to have our best relationship with God now, and that is *understanding*. Understanding is so many actions happening at one moment, together at the same time, such as love, compassion, listening, caring, clarity, healing; those are all parts of understanding. It is a true act of putting everyone's needs in front of your own that pleases God.

Now let's explore the scripture of Proverbs 3:13–17:

> Blessed is the one who finds wisdom, and the one who gets understanding, for the gain from her is better than gain from silver and her profit better than gold. She is more precious than jewels, and nothing you desire can compare with her. Long life is in her right hand; in her left hand are riches and honor. Her ways are ways of pleasantness, and all her paths are peace.

The next element we will explore to have our best relationship with God now is *love*. How can you even begin to explain how amazing and wonderful love is? Love offers so many different ways that allow us to bless others and be blessed. It is what fills the soul with life because it is what you are truly created for: to love others.

Just keep in mind that the only true example of love that has ever existed and will ever exist is Jesus Christ. When you love others so much that you will sacrifice yourself to save them, you can say you know what love is. That means you must love everything through Christ, as He loves you no matter who you are or what you have done.

We will now explore the scripture of 1 Corinthians 13:4–7:

> Love is patient and kind; love does not envy or boast; it is not arrogant or rude. It does not insist on its own way; it is not irritable or resentful; it does not rejoice at wrongdoing, but rejoices with the truth. Love bears all things, believes all things, hopes all things and endures all things.

We conclude this message with the final element to have your best relationship with God now, and that is *acceptance*. Without acceptance, nothing else matters because it will never work out without acceptance. Acceptance is the first activation in your belief system where you take ownership of something and make it part of who you are, like your relationship with God.

First, you must start with the acceptance of your own sins and the repentance of those sins; you must accept forgiveness from Jesus; you must accept being saved and know you are worthy and deserving of it; you must accept the blessings and corrections of your actions as a Christian. But most importantly, you must accept your relationship with God to have your best life now with Him.

Let's keep in mind: acceptance is a two-way street. You are supposed to accept things that are of God in your life but understand the acceptance of ungodly things in your life has consequences. Realize acceptance is the only way to seal your relationship with God now, as you accept His love for you and He accepts your love for Him as a father and a child would.

This concludes part two of "How to Have Your Best Relationship with God Now." To review, so we completely understand what God desires from us as His children:

I pray you have gained in-depth spiritual insight into creating and having the relationship that you want with God and that He wants with you. The next steps are up to you, as He is always waiting for you. There can never be anything between you and God in any form. You must see one another with perfect vision and clarity always so He may know that you are there with Him and that you know He is there with you.

We know that trust is the cornerstone of faith, and without trust, there is no way to have a holy relationship with God or anyone; we must always be understanding, as it is the truest form of putting their needs in front of your own; we are aware that the only true form of love that will ever exist is Jesus Christ inside of us and through us, as He is what creates love within you, and finally, we must have a nature of acceptance in order to be blessed and bless others.

As a final note: we are never too young or old to learn and share with others how to have their best relationship with God. God accepts us no matter where we are or what we have done, which is what you are to do with others to show them the way home that you have found so they can have the best relationship with God and you now and forever.

One of the most important commitments you can make as a Christian is to read your Bible every day. In each message, we will provide you with a few scriptures to look up and read on your own to plant seeds inside of you for a deeper understanding so you can grow closer to Jesus Christ through His written word.

It's time to get your Bible. For your growing with God, scriptures for the message "How to Have Your Best Relationship with God Now" are John 14:23, 1 John 4:7–8, and Romans 8:37–39.

I pray that this message creates a path for you to grow closer to Jesus Christ or meet Him for the first time. If you want to receive the guaranteed passage that He sacrificed Himself on the cross for so you can be saved as a child of God, then become who you are created to be and turn the words you read in this book into action now so you can have eternal life in the kingdom of heaven that is just waiting for you.

Planting Notes:

_____

_____

_____

_____

_____

Welcome to the Poetic Word

(Original Poetry by the Author)

Country Has No Colors

On a summer day,
In a field to nowhere,
I heard a voice
Out of the air:
"I AM here, and I AM everywhere.
Do you have time to share?"

The day flew by
For my new friend and me.
Then he was gone,
As quickly as he came.
He said, "I'll be back again."

I thought to myself,
He is different than me.
That voice came back,
"He's not you; see,

Our country has no colors,
And it's not black and white.
If we all band together,
We'll all be all right.

215

Your skin makes no difference
Like the color of your eyes.
All that matters to me
Is what you are inside."

We must stand forever
Until the end of time,
Just like His Son did
When He gave His life.

Love one another, and you will find
The greatest love you'll have in life.
If you didn't know His name,
It is Jesus Christ.
He will love you wherever you are,
Remove the sins from your heart.
You can have this today
So you know we are just one race.

On a summer day,
In a field to nowhere,
I heard a Voice.

The Battle Cry

When you fall on grace,
Open doors close away,
The sun turns gray,
Smoke fills the inside sky.

As signs of war are day and night,
Over the battles for your life
White flags can be raised;
Either side will take.

One side determines you live;
One side determines you die.

The trumpet sings
The battle cry
Over wrong,
Over right,
Inside your heart,
Inside your mind,
To drown the dark,
To show the light.

Let God's grace shine,
Let God's grace shine,
Let God's grace shine.

It is never over
With Him as your soldier.
He will never surrender;
The sacrifice He gave,

His Son to the grave—
There's no bigger price
For you to be saved.

One side determines you live;
One side determines you die.

He will keep marching on
With the battle cry of His love song.

God Waits

No matter whether they're little or white
Or kept hidden in the dark to hide,
Sin is a lie where you die inside
With each word, your soul fades from His eyes.

With your every delay,
You erase your blessings in life.
Open your heart and open your mind
To shine the light that is inside.

As He waits for your sacrifice,
For you to allow love to come inside,

Patiently He sits right by your side,
His Son, who is there to His right,
Looking through your very eyes,
Hearing every word that comes alive.

God waits,
God waits,
God waits on your love.

The time will come when all is done;
Heaven's door opens no more.
You'll have run your race and died alive
Before you reached the finish line.
You'll never be alone,
If you follow His path
To find your way home,
To know a love you have ever known.

As He waits for your sacrifice,
For you to allow love to come inside,

Patiently He sits by your side,
His Son, who is there to His right,
Looking through your very eyes,
Hearing every word that comes alive.

God waits,
God waits,
God waits on your love.

Patiently He sits by your side,
His Son, who is there to His right,
As He waits for your sacrifice,
For you to allow love to come inside.
God waits.

What Makes Jesus Cry

She was six months shy of sixteen,
Innocent, wild, and free,
Letting the world get
The best of her dreams.

With her every lie,
With her every word,
The light inside
Was no longer hers.

She sacrificed her place
At heaven's gate.

God said it crystal clear,
"Jesus sees you disappear
With your every lie."
Imagine if you were me,
Watching His child die—
This is what makes Jesus cry.

Even though you walked away,
You can come back today
When you give up sin
To be new again.

She heard those words;
Her light flickered once more.
She got on her knees.
She began to pray, "Please, Lord."

She sacrificed her place
At heaven's gate.
God said it crystal clear,
"Jesus sees you disappear
With your every lie."
Imagine if you were me,
Watching His child die—
This is what makes Jesus cry.

"Forgive me, Lord,
Show me the way,
So I do not sin
Or lose my place,"
She spoke those words.
Heaven heard her cry.

God said to her,
"You will not die;
Open the gate and come inside."
This is what makes Jesus cry.

ABOUT THE AUTHOR

Vincent R. Faulkner is a minister, lifetime servant of God, author since age fifteen, award-winning artist, and speaker. His mission of unity is to light a path of passion and pursuit within you for you to grow closer to Jesus Christ or meet Him for the very first time. He has authored several books for children and adults. Vincent lives in Nashville, TN, and has been married for twenty-three years. To learn about his mission of serving God, please visit www.kingsofchrist.com.

CPSIA information can be obtained
at www.ICGtesting.com
Printed in the USA
LVHW011246050422
715339LV00009B/609